Social Justice Language Teacher Education

BILINGUAL EDUCATION & BILINGUALISM
Series Editor: **Nancy H. Hornberger,** *(University of Pennsylvania, USA)* and **Colin Baker** *(Bangor University, Wales, UK)*

Bilingual Education and Bilingualism is an international, multidisciplinary series publishing research on the philosophy, politics, policy, provision and practice of language planning, global English, indigenous and minority language education, multilingualism, multiculturalism, biliteracy, bilingualism and bilingual education. The series aims to mirror current debates and discussions.

Full details of all the books in this series and of all our other publications can be found on http://www.multilingual-matters.com, or by writing to Multilingual Matters, St Nicholas House, 31–34 High Street, Bristol BS1 2AW, UK.

BILINGUAL EDUCATION & BILINGUALISM
Series Editor: Nancy H. Hornberger, *(University of Pennsylvania, USA)* and Colin Baker *(Bangor University, Wales, UK)*

Social Justice Language Teacher Education

Edited by
Margaret R. Hawkins

MULTILINGUAL MATTERS
Bristol • Buffalo • Toronto

This book is dedicated to all of our colleagues working in the fields of education and language studies who, like the authors of these chapters, engage daily in the challenge of transforming educational environments, policies and practices to be more equitable. It is offered in the hope that we continue to create and sustain local, national and global communities working together toward a vision of socially just education everywhere and for all.

Library of Congress Cataloging in Publication Data
A catalog record for this book is available from the Library of Congress.
Social Justice Language Teacher Education/Edited by Margaret R. Hawkins.
Bilingual Education and Bilingualism: 84
Includes bibliographical references and index.
1. Language and languages–Study and teaching–Social aspects. 2. Language teachers–Training of. I. Hawkins, Margaret R.
P53.8.S624 2011
418'.0071–dc22 2011015613

British Library Cataloguing in Publication Data
A catalogue entry for this book is available from the British Library.

ISBN-13: 978-1-84769-423-2 (hbk)
ISBN-13: 978-1-84769-422-5 (pbk)

Multilingual Matters
UK: St Nicholas House, 31–34 High Street, Bristol BS1 2AW, UK.
USA: UTP, 2250 Military Road, Tonawanda, NY 14150, USA.
Canada: UTP, 5201 Dufferin Street, North York, Ontario M3H 5T8, Canada.

Copyright © 2011 Margaret R. Hawkins and authors of individual chapters.

All rights reserved. No part of this work may be reproduced in any form or by any means without permission in writing from the publisher.

The policy of Multilingual Matters/Channel View Publications is to use papers that are natural, renewable and recyclable products, made from wood grown in sustainable forests. In the manufacturing process of our books, and to further support our policy, preference is given to printers that have FSC and PEFC Chain of Custody certification. The FSC and/or PEFC logos will appear on those books where full certification has been granted to the printer concerned.

Typeset by Datapage International Ltd.

Contents

Contributors vii

    Introduction
    Margaret R. Hawkins 1
1 Teacher Education for Social Justice
    Ken Zeichner 7
2 Multimodality, Social Justice and Becoming a 'Really South African' Democracy: Case Studies from Language Classrooms
    Denise Newfield 23
3 Does Intercultural Bilingual Education Open Spaces for Inclusion at Higher Education?
    Mahia Maurial and Moisés Suxo 49
4 Education and Social Justice in Neoliberal Times: Historical and Pedagogical Perspectives from Two Postcolonial Contexts
    Matthew Clarke and Brian Morgan 63
5 Enfranchising the Teacher of English through Action Research: Perspectives on English Language Teacher Education in Uganda
    Robinah Kyeyune 86
6 Dialogic Determination: Constructing a Social Justice Discourse in Language Teacher Education
    Margaret R. Hawkins 102
7 Creating a School Program to Cater to Learner Diversity: A Dialogue between a School Administrator and an Academic
    Franky Poon and Angel Lin 124
8 Working for Social Justice in a Collaborative Action Research Group
    Kelleen Toohey and Bonnie Waterstone 162

Contributors

Matthew Clarke is Senior Lecturer in the School of Education at the University of New South Wales in Sydney. His research interests include teacher formation and teacher identity, as well as critical policy studies. He has published in a range of international journals, including *TESOL Quarterly*, *Asia-Pacific Journal of Education*, *Educational Philosophy and Theory* and *International Journal of Education Development*. His 2008 book, *Language Teacher Identities: Co-Constructing Discourse and Community*, was published by Multilingual Matters.

Margaret R. Hawkins is Professor in the Department of Curriculum and Instruction at the University of Wisconsin – Madison. Her primary research interest, foundationally dedicated to promoting equity for all learners, is in languages and literacies in and out of school, including classroom, home and community-based settings. Her published work examines classroom ecologies, families and schools, and language teacher education. Current projects focus on global digital partnerships for youth, education in Uganda and non-gateway districts' responses to new immigrant and refugee populations. She has published widely and serves as the Chair of the TESOL Research Standing Committee as well as on multiple organizational and editorial boards.

Robinah Kyeyune trained at Makerere University in Uganda and Leeds University and University of Kent in the United Kingdom. She is currently Lecturer on graduate Language Education programs in the School of Education at Makerere University. She has taught English Language and Literature in the secondary school and runs professional development activities for secondary and primary teachers. Her research interests are in the fields of reading, teacher development, group methodologies, language curriculum change and learning support; she has published language teaching textbooks on English as language of instruction.

Angel Lin received her PhD from the Ontario Institute for Studies in Education, University of Toronto, Canada. She is Associate Professor and Associate Dean in the Faculty of Education, University of Hong Kong.

Angel Lin is well-respected for her interdisciplinary scholarship in language and identity studies, bilingual education, classroom discourse analysis, sociocultural theories of second language learning and youth cultural studies. She has published six research books and over 70 research articles. She serves on the editorial boards of a number of international research journals including *Applied Linguistics; International Journal of Bilingual Education and Bilingualism; Language and Education; Journal of Critical Discourse Studies;* and *Pedagogies*.

Mahia Maurial is a Peruvian anthropologist, holding a Master's degree and PhD in Educational Theory and Policy from the Pennsylvania State University. She has worked in the Andes and the Amazon basin of Peru and Bolivia as an advisor and consultant in nongovernmental organizations, international cooperation and government on issues regarding intercultural education and educational policy. She is a coauthor of books about indigenous knowledge and gender. She has been professor at prestigious universities such as the Master's program of PROEIB Andes at the Universidad Mayor de San Simón, Catholic University of Peru and Universidad Peruana de Ciencias Aplicadas.

Brian Morgan is Associate Professor in the Department of English at Glendon College/York University in Toronto, Canada. His academic interests include research and pedagogy on language and identity in English Language Teaching. Research interests include critical multiliteracies and their local and international applications, language teacher education, English for academic purposes, and language policy and planning. He has published in journals such as *TESOL Quarterly; Journal of Language, Identity, and Education; Journal of English for Academic Purposes; Bilingual Education and Bilingualism; Language Policy;* and *Annual Review of Applied Linguistics*. His book, *The ESL Classroom* (1998), is published by the University of Toronto Press.

Denise Newfield is an English teacher educator at the University of the Witwatersrand, South Africa. Her interests span literature, literacy, media, popular culture, pedagogy and curriculum. Her research focuses on how multimodal pedagogies can be used to develop agentive and democratic classrooms. She has investigated the role poetry can play in South Africa's project of educational transformation – in motivating students, developing language competence and reinventing identity – and has published in the fields of English education, multiliteracies and multimodality. She coedited a special edition of *English Studies in Africa*, entitled 'English

Education in Africa' (2006), which contains her award-winning article, 'Mobilising and modalising poetry in a Soweto classroom'.

Franky Poon is the Vice Principal of HKRSS Tai Po Secondary School in Hong Kong. He completed his Master's degree at the Chinese University of Hong Kong, specializing in curriculum development, and is currently a doctoral candidate at the University of Bristol. His work involves educational administration and professional development of teachers, and his interest is in learner diversity and educational leadership.

Yapuchura Suxo Moisés holds an education degree from the Universidad Nacional Mayor de San Marcos (1992–1997) and an MA in Intercultural Bilingual Education from the PROEIB Andes, Universidad Mayor de San Simón in Bolivia (2006). He has been a middle school teacher at Mercedes Indacochea, Lima, Ministry of Education (2000–2010) and Professor at the Universidad Nacional de Educación Enrique Guzmán y Valle, College of Social Sciences and Humanities (2007). His publications include *The Fight for Survival: The Aymara in Lima* (2007) and *The Voice of a Nation: The Aymara of Lima* (2008). He currently promotes the creation of the Aymara intercultural school in Lima.

Kelleen Toohey is Professor and Associate Dean, Academic in the Faculty of Education at Simon Fraser University in British Columbia, Canada. Her recent book with C. Denos, K. Neilson and B. Waterstone, *Collaborative Teacher Research in Multilingual Classrooms* (Multilingual Matters, 2009), documents the activities of the teacher/researcher group with whom she worked. With E. Marshall, she published 'Representing family: Community funds of knowledge, bilingualism and multimodality' (*Harvard Educational Review*, 2010, 80 (2)). Currently interested in multimodal literacies and second language learning, she is engaged in research with such learners and videomaking in Canada, Mexico and India.

Bonnie Waterstone is Lecturer in the Faculty of Education at Simon Fraser University and Coordinator of the International MEd Program in Teaching English as a Foreign or Second Language. Interested in issues of language, identity and difference, she draws on critical, sociocultural and poststructural theories to investigate more equitable research, access to academic discourses, and the politics of English within the current context of increasing internationalization of higher education.

Ken Zeichner is Boeing Professor of Teacher Education and Director of Teacher Education at the University of Washington, Seattle. He is a member of the National Academy of Education and has published and lectured widely on issues of teacher education in the United States. His recent publications include *Teacher Education and the Struggle for Social Justice* (Routledge, Morata), 'Competition, increased surveillance and attacks on multiculturalism: Neo-liberalism and the transformation of teacher education in the U.S.' (*Teaching and Teacher Education*) and 'Rethinking the connections between campus courses and field experiences in university-based teacher education' (*Journal of Teacher Education*).

Introduction

MARGARET R. HAWKINS

Why Social Justice Language Teacher Education?

There is currently an increase in focus, within the field of education worldwide, on globalization and particularly on its inherent movement of people across national and international borders. In response to this movement, educators are grappling with defining 'best practices' for teaching immigrant, migrant and refugee students. Simultaneously, many countries that are home to multiple indigenous language and cultural groups are attempting to broaden and unify the reach and scope of education, resulting in the provision of education in languages other than students' home languages. With increased visibility of language issues come increasing regional and national interests in setting policies and in ensuring accountability in educational outcomes for students who do not speak the dominant language of the communities in which they live. Thus there is a demand for teachers to know how to adequately support students to learn the language of instruction in schools, although there is little agreement in the educational literature on how best to do so. What is clear, however, is that virtually *all* teachers, regardless of geographic location or area of expertise, must be prepared to teach students from diverse linguistic and cultural backgrounds, whereas historically language teacher education was considered the domain of those preparing to be 'language' teachers.

The language teacher education literature primarily falls into two distinct categories: (1) scholars and educators who focus on issues of language, including grammar, function, structure and usage; and (2) those who focus on linguistically and culturally responsive pedagogies. This stems, in part, from the trajectory of the ways in which language learning and teaching has been approached historically, moving from a view of language as a set of words and structures governed by particular principles and stored in the mind (a psycholinguistic approach) through a view of language as a tool for meaning-making (a communicative approach) to a view of meaning-making as situated in specific social encounters that take place in specific places at specific times between specific people (a sociocultural approach), and ultimately to a view of situated language usage that is shaped through pervasive social, cultural and political ideologies and forces that serve to empower some people while marginalizing others (a critical approach). While language teacher preparation often takes into account competencies from the first category identified above – ensuring that teachers know something about grammar, structure and function – issues that align with sociocultural perspectives fall within the second category and are embodied in culturally and linguistically responsive pedagogy. Rarely are teachers of students who are not being schooled in their home language, through preservice or in-service preparation or professional development, provided the opportunity to explore the impact of sociocultural issues on the language, literacy and academic learning of their students. And almost never are critical issues and approaches part of language teacher education practices (although see Hawkins & Norton, 2009, for several examples of exceptions).

In this volume, we call for a turn to social justice language teacher education. While 'critical' language teacher education puts the focus squarely on societal inequities often based on differences vis-à-vis race, class, gender, language, dis/ability and ethnicity and calls for educators (and indeed everybody) to understand how positioning within those categories leads to inequitable distribution of goods and resources, including education, a social justice turn highlights teachers' responsibility to serve as agents of social change. This aligns with current literature in mainstream teacher education, where scholars advocate for social justice teacher education (e.g. Cochran-Smith, 2004; McDonald, 2005; McDonald & Zeichner, 2009; Zeichner, 2009). A social justice approach not only shifts understandings of language learning, teaching and usage, acknowledges inequities in educational landscapes and envisions more just social futures, but redefines the roles of teachers in effecting change.

As noted above, there is much educational rhetoric, in policy and scholarship, about 'best practices' for serving English learners. As may be clear, the conceptual frames we utilize to understand what language teaching, learning and use is and entails shape our program designs, curricula and practices. Those of us who adopt a sociocultural, critical and/or social justice approach (they are not the same, but they are not mutually exclusive) are not apt to buy into the notion of 'best practices' at all. We believe that learning and teaching (including but not limited to language learning and teaching) occur in specific situated contexts and are contingent on the time, place and participants in specific interactions that constitute the learning events, all of which is, in part, shaped by larger societal and institutional discourses. Thus curriculum and pedagogy must be responsive to local contexts and contingencies. However, if we are not advocating for a stable, fixed set of programs and practices, what do we advocate for? How can educators know how to approach the design and implementation of education for English learners?

The Book

Authors in this book explore just those questions. What is social justice language teacher education, and what might it look like? In the opening chapter, Zeichner articulates a view of a social justice approach to teacher education. In subsequent chapters, authors from diverse geographic locales offer theorized accounts of their social justice language teacher education practices, aligning with aspects of Zeichner's vision. These accounts are not meant to be prescriptive but to demonstrate how social justice language teacher education has been taken up across the globe to respond to local contexts and circumstances. Chapters address language teacher preparation at all levels – preservice, in-service and professional development; formal and informal; graduate, undergraduate and non-matriculated – and represent university-based programs and classes as well as non-university-based educational configurations and modes. Chapters also define 'language teacher' in various ways: as grade-level or subject-area teachers in places where the language that is the medium of instruction is not the language of the community and students' homes; as grade-level or subject-area teachers whose students include both native speakers and nonnative speakers of the language of instruction; as teachers being prepared to teach the dominant language of the community as a subject area to nonnative speakers; and as those being prepared to teach a language as a foreign language in communities where it is not the dominant language.

While cross-cutting themes, issues and challenges are evident, there is no panacea offered. In fact, while many of the authors point to what they consider to be powerful components of practice, such as collaboration, dialogue, reflection and working to empower/legitimize teachers, they point equally to the challenge and tensions of doing this work within the context of societal and institutional power structures. There are no easy solutions to preparing teachers to provide equitable educations to students who are not aligned with dominant language and literacy practices in schools and communities. Each author offers a look at their programs and practices as they are informed by their beliefs, discussing their efforts and attendant challenges.

The book begins, in Chapter 1, with an articulation by Ken Zeichner of key elements of, and challenges in, social justice teacher education. In 'Teacher Education for Social Justice', Zeichner explicates the need for such an approach and situates it within the current professional teacher education literature. He describes programs designed to align with a social justice approach and discusses pitfalls and tensions.

In 'Multimodality, Social Justice and Becoming a "Really South African" Democracy: Case Studies from Language Classrooms' (Chapter 2), Denise Newfield examines social justice in education in postapartheid South Africa. She portrays the current educational landscape and policies and discusses how she and her colleagues, through a shared vision, are attempting to transform teacher education in her university. She calls for a multimodal approach to social justice language teacher education to 'form the foundation of a semiotics that is strongly grounded in the social' (p. 25) and to articulate with South African ways of knowing and communicating. She then describes three projects from South African classrooms that utilize a multimodal approach in the service of social justice language (and language teacher) education.

Mahia Maurial and Moisés Suxo, in Chapter 3, 'Does Intercultural Bilingual Education Open Spaces for Inclusion at Higher Education?' provide a history of Intercultural Bilingual Education as socioculturally situated in South America and compare and contrast it to social justice teacher education. They then describe the Peruvian university program in which they work, analyzing systemically, programmatically, socially and practically how it does and does not align with the indigenous ways of knowing, learning and relating that its indigenous students bring to the program. They discuss the role of research and suggest recommendations for future directions.

In Chapter 4, 'Education and Social Justice in Neoliberal Times: Historical and Pedagogical Perspectives from Two Postcolonial Contexts', Matthew Clarke and Brian Morgan explicate how neoliberal concerns with effectiveness and accountability encourage narrow understandings of education and teaching and lead to reform agendas that do not promote social justice. They provide examples from their respective contexts in Australia and Canada, situating them historically, and illustrate how they each, in their own contexts, provide their students with linguistic tools to analyze and challenge contemporary neoliberal discourses.

Chapter 5 turns the social justice lens on language teacher education in Uganda. In 'Enfranchising the Teacher of English through Action Research: Perspectives on English Language Teacher Education in Uganda', Robinah Kyeyune situates readers in the local language and English-medium educational environments in Uganda. She discusses current policies and programs for schools and current practices in language teacher preparation. Through an analysis of teacher training programs, she points to inequities in the teaching of English and in the teaching of teachers, locating these primarily in hierarchical relations of power within institutions. She calls for critical inquiry from teacher trainers, and for action research to be implemented as part of the teacher preparation program in order to empower teachers to see themselves as agents for change and to ultimately change the educational landscape.

In Chapter 6, 'Dialogic Determination: Constructing a Social Justice Discourse in Language Teacher Education', Margaret R. Hawkins offers a rationale for social justice language teacher education, grounding her discussion in current educational discourses around teaching English learners in the United States. She describes a language teacher education program built on principles of social justice and conducts an empirical analysis of the effectiveness of an English as a second language methods course for K–12 teachers designed to fully integrate a social justice perspective. The analysis portrays some of the tensions and struggles in implementing social justice language teacher education and points to critical issues for exploration.

Chapter 7 presents a contextualized e-mail exchange between a school vice principal and a university faculty member in Hong Kong. In 'Creating a School Program to Cater for Learner Diversity: A Dialogue between a School Administrator and an Academic', Franky Poon and Angel Lin explore the complicated issues around providing instruction, including a remedial English resource class, for special education students in Franky's school, in an effort to provide them a socially just and equitable education. The dialogue functions to provide scaffolding for Franky's explorations and efforts but also is educational for Angel; they call for professional development to intersect academic and practitioner spaces.

The final chapter (Chapter 8), 'Working for Social Justice in a Collaborative Action Research Group', by Kelleen Toohey and Bonnie Waterstone, portrays the power of collaborative inquiry groups as a form of professional development. After introducing the reader to the histories, goals, composition and activities of the TARG (Teacher Action Research Group) group in which the authors participated, they provide a rationale for action research in the service of social justice work. Then, through detailed description and analysis of the activities and interactions of the group, they portray the tensions and challenges of collaborative inquiry when participants have differing goals and interests shaped by their differing positions across different institutional domains and discourses. They problematize 'communities who work for social change' while portraying how such 'educative spaces' hold promise for social justice transformation in education.

Authors hope that readers find the chapters informative and that our work may, perhaps, through illuminating what a social justice lens has to offer to language teacher education, be generative of ideas that may be taken up and applied, in locally responsive ways, in readers' own contexts.

References

Cochran-Smith, M. (2004) *Walking the Road: Race, Diversity and Social Justice in Teacher Education*. New York: Teachers College Press.

Hawkins, M. and Norton, B. (2009) Critical language teacher education. In J. Richards. and A. Burns (eds) *The Cambridge Guide To Second Language Teacher Education*. Cambridge, UK: Cambridge University Press.

McDonald, M. and Zeichner, K. (2009) Social justice teacher education. In W. Ayers, T. Quinn and D. Stovall (eds) *Handbook of Social Justice in Education*. New York: Routledge.

McDonald, M.A. (2005) The integration of social justice in teacher education. *Journal of Teacher Education* 56 (5), 418–435.

Zeichner, K. (2009) *Teacher Education and the Struggle for Social Justice*. New York: Routledge.

Chapter 1
Teacher Education for Social Justice[1]

KEN ZEICHNER

The focus of this chapter is on an approach to teacher education that has come to be known as teacher education for social justice. Although various labels have been attached to this approach over the years, such as social reconstructionist teacher education, antiracist teacher education, critical teacher education and social reconstructionist multicultural teacher education, social justice teacher education (SJTE) seems to have become the label of choice among college and university teacher educators in recent years (e.g. Cochran-Smith, 1999; McDonald & Zeichner, 2009; Michelli & Keiser, 2005; Solomon *et al.*, 2007; Zeichner, 2009).

SJTE aims to respond to preparing teachers to teach in ways that contribute to a lessening of the inequalities that exist in school systems throughout the world between children of the poor and children of the middle and wealthy classes, and the injustices that exist in societies beyond systems of schooling – in access to shelter, food, healthcare, transportation, access to meaningful work that pays a living wage, and so on. The uncertainty that characterizes the current context is related to the uncertain future this planet faces if these injustices persist. We continue today to see widening gaps in education and income between the haves and have-nots in every society.

In current times, SJTE also aims to prepare teachers to teach in societies where increasingly narrow and punitive forms of accountability have been thrust upon schools and teacher education institutions that are often inconsistent with educators' own views about what they are trying to accomplish (Hamel & Merz, 2005; Johnson *et al.*, 2005; Sirotnik, 2001). Teachers and others who work in schools do not object to being held accountable for their work, but to the narrow forms of accountability that they are required to meet (Ingersoll, 2003). The 'No Child Left Behind'(NCLB) Act in the United States, for example, which has required high stakes testing during many years of schooling, has captured a large share of the insufficient resources that have been given to public education after the military and the corporations have taken their shares. Public education systems throughout the world are underfunded and teachers are underpaid everywhere (UNESCO, 1998). Current accountability mandates often adopt a punitive stance toward schools and blame teachers and school administrators for the problems of the society (Dahlstrom, 2006; Reimers, 1994).

In some cases, such as in large urban school districts in the United States and in many classrooms throughout the developing world, the press for high stakes testing has been combined with efforts to minimize opportunities for teachers to exercise their judgment in their classrooms as curriculum is scripted and prescribed (Robertson, 2008; Samoff, 1999; Sleeter, 2008; Tatto, 2006; Torres, 2000).

In the United States, for example, a high government official in the federal education department spoke in a meeting of teacher educators and foundation staff about the need to prepare 'good enough teachers', just good enough to follow a scripted curriculum and be trained in prescribed teaching practices that are allegedly based on research. He and others in the Bush administration claimed that tightly monitoring teachers' actions, scripting the curriculum and intensifying standardized testing with serious consequences for schools and teachers related to examination results will lead to rising levels of educational quality and a narrowing of the achievement gaps between different groups.[2]

The argument has been made that many children in US public schools, particularly poor children and children of color, have less access to fully qualified teachers who have completed a teacher education program and that these 'good enough teachers' who are trained to follow directions but not to think and exercise their judgment are better than teachers who are just pulled in off the street with no preparation at all.

This same argument has been made in many developing countries that also struggle to give all students access to teachers who have completed a teacher education program at the postsecondary level. With increased access to basic education and in some countries to secondary education, and with the implementation of neoliberal economic policies that have resulted in drastic reductions in public expenditures in many countries (e.g. Carnoy, 1995; Klees, 2002), it has become increasingly difficult to provide qualified teachers for every child (Villegas Reimers & Reimers, 1996). Some say that providing a fully qualified teacher to all learners around the world is an unrealistic goal unless we move to a more cost-effective training of teacher technicians. Consequently, many nations have moved toward establishing 'fast track' programs that get people into the classroom as quickly as possible, oftentimes with little prior preparation (e.g. Baines, 2006; Hinchey & Cadiero-Kaplan, 2005).

I find it interesting that many of these government officials who advocate 'good enough teachers' apparently do not find these teachers good enough for their own children whom they often send to private schools. There is a clear gap in many countries between children who have access to fully qualified teachers and those who do not, which is connected to social class and immigrant status (e.g. Peske & Haycock, 2006). Dewey (1929) asserted that 'what the best and wisest parent wants for his own child that must the community want for all of its children'. Whatever one thinks about the role of teachers and schooling, one should be willing to subject one's own children and grandchildren to what one advocates for other people's children. If this one principle were followed by policymakers around the world, we would probably find a lot smaller gaps in the quality of education experienced by different children.

Despite all of the forces that are seeking to maintain unjust and unequal societies and educational systems, dedicated and talented teachers, administrators and others continue to work against the grain in progressive ways that contribute to greater social justice through public education. One goal of SJTE has been to make this kind of teaching possible for more students.

Teacher Education Reform Agendas

Over the years, I have had a particular interest in trying to make sense of the different purposes and practices associated with calls for reform in teacher education and particularly with what has come to be called SJTE. From the very beginning of my career in education, I saw my efforts as a teacher connected to efforts to bring about greater equity in schooling and society, providing individuals like me who attended a large urban public school system with the same high quality of education that is routinely available to others who come from more economically advantaged backgrounds. I chose to enter teaching in the first place as an alternative to fighting in what many of us thought was an unjust war in Vietnam and all of my public school teaching was done in schools in predominately low-income African American communities (Zeichner, 1995). Much of my research over the years has focused on studying efforts within my own teacher education program and in other programs to prepare teachers who will contribute to a more equal and just world.

I have made a number of attempts over the years to try and identify the links between specific proposals for teacher education reform and broader traditions of thought that have existed over time, the most recent of which identified three broad strands of teacher education reform that I think exist in some form or another throughout the world: the professionalization agenda, the deregulation agenda and the social justice agenda (see Zeichner, 2003). I am not going to go into the differences between these three agendas here, other than to say that teacher education programs throughout the world are influenced by all of them simultaneously. The professionalization agenda has led to the conversion of many teacher education programs throughout the world to performance assessment based on a set of teaching standards (Freeman-Moir & Scott, 2007). The deregulation agenda has challenged the monopoly that colleges and universities have had on teacher education and has resulted in the adoption of many fast track certification programs that seek to put teachers in schools in places where it is hard to attract them and keep them there. The deregulators want to subject teacher education to market forces, and according to this neoliberal view, competition will enhance quality (Walsh, 2004; Weiner, 2007).

Social Justice Teacher Education

The third and final reform agenda is the social justice agenda, which incorporates various aspects of what has been referred to as social reconstructionist, multicultural, antiracist, bilingual and inclusive education. Although SJTE draws on aspects of these strands of teacher education, it is distinguished from them by its focus on helping to bring about broad-scale social change in the social, economic, political and educational spheres of society (see Kailin, 2002; McDonald & Zeichner, 2009). I will outline the arguments made by advocates of this agenda, the variety of teacher education practices that have been situated within the broad social justice umbrella and then offer my constructive critique of this line of reform, not as an outsider but as one who is involved in this very work every day.

The Goals of Social Justice Teacher Education

SJTE places the recruiting of a more diverse teaching force and the preparation of all teachers to teach all students at the center of attention. It goes beyond a celebration of diversity to attempt to prepare teachers who are willing and able to work within and outside of their classrooms to change the inequities that exist in both schooling and the wider society (McDonald & Zeichner, 2009). There is an acknowledgment of the social and political dimensions of teaching along with its other dimensions and recognition of teachers' contributions to the life chances of their students.

SJTE is supported by a substantial research literature that identifies the attributes and strategies of what has come to be called culturally responsive teaching. Although work remains to be done to clarify and elaborate the elements of what teachers need to know, be able to do and be like to successfully teach in today's public schools, the work of scholars such as Jackie Jordan Irvine, Gloria Ladson-Billings, Geneva Gay, Ana Maria Villegas, Tamara Lucas, Luis Moll and Sonia Nieto has been remarkably consistent in the elements of good teaching they identify (e.g. Gay, 2000; Irvine & Armento, 2001; Ladson-Billings, 1995; Villegas & Lucas, 2002).

Following is one example of the knowledge, skills and commitments that have emerged from this research literature on culturally responsive teaching offered by Villegas and Lucas (2002).

(1) Is socioculturally conscious – recognizes that there are multiple ways of perceiving reality that are influenced by one's location in the social order.
(2) Has affirming view of students from diverse backgrounds, seeing resources in learning in all students rather than viewing differences as problems to overcome.
(3) Sees himself or herself as both responsible for and capable of bringing about educational change that will make schools responsive to all students.
(4) Understands how learners construct knowledge and is capable of promoting learners' knowledge construction.
(5) Knows about the lives of his or her students (including funds of knowledge in their communities).
(6) Uses his or her knowledge about students' lives to design instruction that builds on what they already know while stretching them beyond the familiar.

SJTE is not a new phenomenon. For example, in our 1991 book *Teacher Education and the Social Conditions of Schooling*, Dan Liston and I outlined a number of efforts in the United States beginning in the 1930s, including New College at Teachers College in New York City from 1932 to 1939 where students were given course credit for participating in political demonstrations. The emergence of social foundations courses in teacher education programs in the 1930s was another early example of SJTE in the United States (Liston & Zeichner, 1991).

These examples and others, such as the Putney Graduate School of Teacher Education from 1950 to 1964 recently studied by Carol Rodgers, consciously sought to apply to teacher education the idea that teachers could be prepared to be leaders of social reconstruction. In addition to preparing teachers to work in classrooms with their students, they sought to connect teachers' education with broader social change movements (Rodgers, 2006).

For example, the Putney program included students living together in mixed-race groups and studying and meeting with leading voices in the US Civil Rights movement. As part of their studies, students traveled together in vans for periods of several weeks at a time and reflected upon these experiences. These study tours were journeys usually to areas of the south where struggles for social justice were going on. The goal, according to Rodgers, was to insert their multiracial groups of teacher education students into the midst of social problems such as racism and strip mining and to introduce them to responses to these problems such as the Highlander School, the Montgomery Bus Boycott, citizenship schools and cooperative communities. Although these programs and others have been part of North American teacher education since the 1930s, they have always been marginal to the mainstream of teacher education.

From the beginning of SJTE efforts the goal has been to educate teachers who would assume leadership roles in the reconstruction of society toward greater equity in opportunities and outcomes among the different groups that make up the society. Educating teachers to be leaders in social reconstruction would then lead to teachers educating their students to become active in bringing about social change. A paper in the journal *Social Frontier* in 1938 nicely captures the logic here:

> The duty of the teachers colleges is clear. They must furnish over a period of years a staff of workers for the public schools who thoroughly understand the social, economic, and political problems with which this country is faced, who are zealous in the improvement of present conditions and who are capable of educating citizens disposed to study social problems earnestly, think critically about them and act in accord with their noblest impulses. (Brown, 1938: 328)

Tensions in Social Justice Teacher Education

There have been a number of tensions that have been part of SJTE programs since their inception. For example, there was a vigorous debate among SJTE advocates that continues today about whether the goal, as Counts (1932) had argued in 'Dare the Schools Build a New Social

Order', should be to indoctrinate future teachers in the principles of a new society or whether it should be to educate teachers in the skills and habits of critical analysis without proposing a specific alternative vision of society.

There has also been a tension between the goals of SJTE educators who want to prepare teachers to be leaders of social change and the goals of at least some future teachers who do not want to assume this role. Finally, there has also been a tension between the academic discourse about teaching for social change and the connection of this discourse to the communities where the work is to be carried out. Basically, ceding college and university academics the preferential right of interpretation about what counts as SJTE is inconsistent with the basic tenets of social justice education, where teachers and community members whose children attend the public schools would participate in significant ways in the process of shaping and then educating teachers. Some, including myself, have argued that teacher education needs to be situated not in colleges or universities or schools but in a hybrid culture where the preferential right of interpretation is more democratically shared (Gorodetsky & Barak, 2008; Zeichner, in press).

Dimensions of Variation in Social Justice Teacher Education

There are various ways to distinguish the work that has gone on for some years under the labels of social reconstructionist, antiracist, multicultural and SJTE. For example, some programs attempt to infuse a social justice perspective throughout the entire teacher education curriculum, and one can see in these programs how a general set of standards and goals with a social justice focus are elaborated and defined within the various components of the program.

Although this infusion approach has been the preferred approach in the literature on SJTE for many years, it is still very common and is probably the dominant approach to isolate attention to SJ issues in one or a few courses that are often taught by the 'multicultural faculty' who are often faculty of color (e.g. Moule, 2005).

Issues such as diversity, social justice and equity, like many other aspects of the teacher education curriculum, have suffered from fragmentation and the lack of curricular cohesiveness that has historically plagued teacher education in colleges and universities. This fragmentation is a consequence of a variety of things, including the low status of teacher education on many university campuses, the lack of incentives for faculty to work on program development and betterment and the lack of expertise about social justice issues among teacher education faculty (Labaree, 2004).

Another dimension along which SJTE programs vary is the degree to which they emphasize interacting with cultures and efforts to build social justice as opposed to studying about cultures and social justice work. Although all teacher education programs include at least some direct field experience in schools and sometimes in communities, programs vary as to how much their students are put in contact with students and adults from different backgrounds and the nature of these interactions. For example, some programs emphasize reading and discussing material about issues of race, diversity and equity with very little direct experience with others different than oneself, while others include substantial work in communities where student teachers are positioned as learners rather than as saviors.

For several years, I studied a program in Chicago where students lived together in a multicultural and socioeconomically diverse neighborhood and where a significant amount of their time was spent in planned interactions with community activists and neighborhood residents (Zeichner & Melnick, 1996). Barbara Seidl's current work in Columbus, OH, where student teachers are partnered with equal-status adults in an African American church as part of their program, is another example of shifting the center of gravity of teacher education from the university campus to communities (Seidl & Friend, 2002).

A final dimension along which SJTE programs vary is the degree to which programs are models of the culturally responsive and activist approaches that they advocate for their students. On the one hand, programs may be responsive to the diverse perspectives and experiences brought to their preparation by their students, the needs of students of color may be addressed and students in such programs may not only be positioned as the educators of white students about diversity. The students are actively involved in their own education, and faculty who actually work in the program on a regular basis work closely with both their students and cooperating school staff.

On the other hand, SJTE is transmitted to students in many programs in an additive manner with little regard for the varied backgrounds and experiences of the students, and student teachers are put in the position of being passive recipients about a culturally responsive approach to teaching and working actively for social justice, but they do not get to experience it in their education for teaching. Conklin (2008) has argued that teacher educators who claim to work for social justice need to model the same kind of caring, compassionate and responsive relationships with their students as they hope to foster in P-12 classrooms.

Social Justice Teacher Education Practices

The teacher education literature has illuminated some of the practices in teacher education programs that teacher educators are using under the umbrella of SJTE to develop greater intercultural sensitivity and teaching competence among prospective teachers. I have been attempting to document these for a number of years now and to assess the extent to which there is an empirical warrant for the claims that are made about some of these practices. These include the following:

(1) Admissions policies that screen applicants on the basis of a variety of factors including their commitment to teach all students and other personal characteristics related to intercultural teaching competence (e.g. Villegas & Lucas, 2004).
(2) Modifying teacher standards and assessments to more clearly focus on aspects of culturally responsive teaching (e.g. Vavrus, 2002).
(3) Helping prospective teachers to develop a clearer sense of their own ethnic and cultural identities and their own social location and knowledge of how various forms of privilege operate in their society (e.g. white and English language privilege) (e.g. Marx, 2006).
(4) Helping prospective teachers to deeply examine their own attitudes and assumptions about those who are different from themselves in various ways (e.g. Banks *et al.*, 2005).
(5) Building high expectations for all students (e.g. exposure to successful examples of teaching underserved students) (Zeichner, 1996).
(6) Carefully monitoring and analyzing field experiences in culturally diverse schools and communities, including cultural immersion experiences in which student teachers live in culturally different communities (Zeichner, in press).
(7) Using noncertified adults in communities as paid teacher educators teaching prospective teachers cultural and linguistic knowledge (e.g. community panels) (e.g. Mahan, 1982).
(8) Teaching prospective teachers how to learn about their students' families and communities and how to translate this learning into culturally responsive teaching practices (e.g. incorporating funds of knowledge from communities) (e.g. Lucas, 2005).

(9) Incorporating a commitment to diversity in program and institutional contexts and not just in individual courses (e.g. Ladson-Billings, 1999).
(10) Recruiting, supporting and retaining more diverse teacher education faculty.

It should be noted that there are a number of different instructional methods used in the context of doing all these things such as action research, case studies and portfolios. These methods can be used to serve a variety of purposes and are not necessarily a sign of SJTE. It is the purposes toward which these methods are used and how they are used that is important to understand.

Problems with Social Justice Teacher Education

Despite the important contributions made by advocates of the social justice agenda for reform in these dangerous times, there are a number of problems in my view that have weakened its impact. First, most of what has been done by advocates of SJTE has been done at the level of the teacher education classroom as teacher educators have introduced activities and experiences into their programs.

Both the professionalization and deregulation agendas have addressed the broader structures of teaching and teacher education and, although one may not agree with their stances on issues, they have framed the discourse among policymakers. It is clear that any solution to the problems of inequity in education will need to address the broader structures within which the work is embedded. The focus of SJTE work at the local level of individuals or groups of teacher educators within programs will not greatly impact the larger structures that shape teaching and the larger societal problem of inequality in education provision and outcomes.

A second major limitation of the social justice agenda is the lack of capacity among teacher educators to do the job that needs to be done. For example, although many teacher educators have had teaching experience, not many have had successful experience as teachers in the kinds of high poverty, diverse and segregated education systems that exist today (Zeichner, 1996) and there is generally very little deliberate preparation and induction and continuing professional development available to faculty in relation to the teacher education aspect of their positions (Cochran-Smith, 2003).

Also, despite what we know from research about the value of closely connecting teacher education programs to diverse communities and about employing community members as teacher educators, many programs continue to operate today as if the task of preparing teachers who will work for social justice is primarily a matter of sitting in university classrooms and reading and discussing things or of placing student teachers and interns in culturally different schools for their field experiences.

Another problem with SJTE is that it has almost exclusively, according to the literature, focused on the transformation of white teachers to teach students of color living in poverty instead of the goal of preparing all teachers to teach all students. A whole literature has emerged in recent years documenting the failure of teacher education to address the learning needs of prospective teachers of color in dominant white institutions (e.g. Montecinos, 2004; Villegas & Davis, 2008). This literature argues that although growing up as a person of color causes individuals to experience things differently from a white person (e.g. racism), one cannot equate being a person of color with being an effective teacher. The task of teacher education needs to be reframed in this view to one of addressing the needs of all prospective teachers to teach for social justice and not framed exclusively from a white perspective (Sleeter, 2001).

Also, much of the work that has occurred under the label of multicultural teacher education has focused on issues of race, gender and social class and has ignored the massive immigration going on around the world and the preparation of teachers to teach increasing numbers of dominant language learners in public school systems throughout the world. According to the research, the preparation of all teachers should include content related to the components of language, the process of language acquisition and teaching strategies for teaching dominant language learners (Lucas & Grinberg, 2008). In the United States, preparation to teach English Language Learners is often the most negatively rated item in follow-up surveys of teacher education program graduates, and issues of language diversity have been segregated, with an applied linguistics component only being offered for the most part to ESL and bilingual teachers. Also, in the United States there is almost no research outside of ESL and bilingual education on the preparation of teachers with regard to issues of language diversity.

Conclusion

Despite the problems that I have been pointing out in this essay, SJTE has made remarkable strides in becoming part of the everyday discourse in teacher education throughout the world. The success of SJTE in becoming the new slogan in teacher education, while problematic from a certain perspective, should be applauded in these times when assaults are being made by the right on multicultural education of any kind, let alone a version that seeks to promote greater social justice.

The success of SJTE in becoming mainstreamed into the everyday discourse of teacher education can become a serious problem in the long run however (like it was for reflective teaching in the 1980s and 1990s), when what is done under the name of social justice does not truly involve the forming of linkages inside and outside of education aimed at working for broad social change, and when it is conducted in isolation from teachers and communities that are working toward the same purposes.

One of the things that needs to be done (McDonald, 2005; Michelli & Keiser, 2005) that I have not discussed in this chapter is to clarify what is meant by social justice in teacher education programs that use this as a frame. There are clearly different conceptions of justice that range at a basic level from things such as distinguishing between equitable opportunities and equitable outcomes to various theoretical frameworks that talk about an equitable redistribution of resources or a respect for group differences (McDonald, 2005). My own view of justice in SJTE pays attention to both its distributive and relational aspects and is similar to the position advocated by Fraser (1997).

In the end, the inequities in a country's public schooling are closely linked with gaps in access to jobs that pay a living wage, housing and transportation at reasonable prices, healthcare, and so on. Although schooling and teacher education can play an important role in addressing these inequities and injustices, they must be viewed as only one part of a more comprehensive plan for reform of societies. Without the broader political work that needs to be done at many levels to change the ways in which societies' resources are allocated (e.g. for wars, prisons and sports stadiums instead of schools and education), SJTE will be of little consequence in the long run (Berliner, 2005).

SJTE needs to move beyond the largely academic discourse on university campuses that it has become and begin to provide more practical tools to go along with the conceptual lenses. In order to do this, strong linkages need to be formed with the teachers and administrators in our schools who are doing good work and with parents and others in local communities who are working for social change to bring about greater justice within schools and in the broader society (see Zeichner, 2006).

These alliances need to be very different from the kind of 'university expert passes knowledge to the uninformed teachers and citizens' model that has characterized faculty interactions outside of the academy in many places. We need more attention by those of us in universities to what we can learn from teachers and parents about educating teachers who will be advocates for social justice, and to link our efforts within the education arena to broader social movements.

In the end, we should not settle for anything less for anyone's children than we would want for our own children. Good enough teachers should not be good enough for anyone's children, and the lack of access to the basic necessities needed to live a life with dignity by anyone on this planet should not be tolerated. These are the most fundamental issues that teacher education faces in the years ahead.

Notes

1. This chapter is based on a keynote talk given at a conference sponsored by the Faculty of Education of Simon Fraser University, 'Teacher Development: The Key to the 21st Century', Vancouver, Canada, March 2006.
2. This meeting was held at the Carnegie Foundation for the Advancement of Teaching in June 2002.

References

Baines, L. (2006) Deconstructing teacher certification. *Phi Delta Kappan* 88 (4), 326–329.
Banks, J., Cochran-Smith, M., Moll, L., Richert, A., Zeichner, K., LePage, P., Darling-Hammond, L. and Duffy, H. (2005) Teaching diverse learners. In L. Darling-Hammond and J. Bransford (eds) *Preparing Teachers for a Changing World* (pp. 232–274). San Francisco: Jossey-Bass.
Berliner, D. (2005) Our impoverished view of educational reform. *Teachers College Record*. On WWW at http://www.tcrecord.org. Accessed 19.8.05.
Brown, H. (1938) A challenge to teachers' colleges. *Social Frontier* 4 (37), 327–329.
Carnoy, M. (1995) Structural adjustment and the changing face of education. *International Labor Review* 134 (6), 653–674.
Cochran-Smith, M. (1999) Learning to teach for social justice. In G. Griffin (ed.) *The Education of Teachers: Ninety-Eight Yearbook of the National Society for the Study of Education* (pp. 114–144). Chicago: University of Chicago Press.
Cochran-Smith, M. (2003) Learning and unlearning: The education of teacher educators. *Teaching and Teacher Education* 19, 5–28.
Conklin, H. (2008) Modeling compassion in critical, justice-oriented teacher education. *Harvard Educational Review* 78 (4), 652–674.
Counts, G. (1932) *Dare the Schools Build a New Social Order?* New York: John Day Co.
Dahlstrom, L. (2006) *The Liberal Virus and the False Opportunity Promise in Third World Education*. Umea, Sweden: Global South Network, Umea University. On WWW at http://alfa.ped.umu.se/projekt/globalsouthnetwork. Accessed 14.5.11.
Dewey, J. (1929) *The Sources of a Science of Education*. New York: Liveright.

Fraser, N. (1997) *Justice Interruptus: Critical Reflections on the 'Post-Socialist' Condition*. New York: Routledge.
Freeman-Moir, J. and Scott, A. (eds) (2007) *Shaping the Future: Critical Essays on Teacher Education*. Rotterdam: Sense Publishers.
Gay, G. (2000) *Culturally Responsive Teaching: Theory, Research, and Practice*. New York: Teachers College Press.
Gorodetsky, M. and Barak, J. (2008) The educational-cultural edge: A participative learning environment for co-emergence of personal and institutional growth. *Teaching and Teacher Education* 24, 1907–1918.
Hamel, F. and Merz, C. (2005) Reforming accountability: A preservice program wrestles with mandated reform. *Journal of Teacher Education* 56 (2), 157–167.
Hinchey, P. and Cadiero-Kaplan, K. (2005) The future of teacher education and teaching: Another piece of the privatization puzzle. *Journal for Critical Educational Policy Studies* 3 (2). On WWW at http://www.jceps.com. Accessed 17.9.07.
Ingersoll, R. (2003) *Who Controls Teachers' Work: Power and Accountability in America's Schools*. Cambridge, MA: Harvard University Press.
Irvine, J.J. and Armento, B. (2001) *Culturally Responsive Teaching: Lesson Planning for Elementary and Middle Grades*. Boston: McGraw-Hill.
Johnson, D., Johnson, B., Farenga, S. and Ness, D. (2005) *Trivializing Teacher Education: The Accreditation Squeeze*. Lanham, MD: Roman & Littlefield.
Kailin, J. (2002) *Antiracist Education*. Lanham, MD: Roman & Littlefield.
Klees, S. (2002) World Bank education policy: New rhetoric, old ideology. *International Journal of Educational Development* 22, 451–474.
Labaree, D. (2004) *The Trouble with Ed Schools*. New Haven, CT: Yale University Press.
Ladson-Billings, G. (1995) Toward a theory of culturally relevant pedagogy. *American Educational Research Journal* 32 (3), 465–491.
Ladson-Billings, G. (1999) Preparing teachers for diverse student populations: A critical race theory perspective. In A. Iran-Najed and P. David Pearson (eds) *Review of Research in Education* (Vol. 24, pp. 211–247). Washington, DC: American Educational Research Association.
Liston, D. and Zeichner, K. (1991) *Teacher Education and the Social Conditions of Schooling*. New York: Routledge.
Lucas, T. (2005) Fostering a commitment to social justice through service learning in a teacher education course. In N. Michelli and D.L. Keiser (eds) *Teacher Education for Democracy and Social Justice* (pp. 167–188). New York: Routledge.
Lucas, T. and Grinberg, J. (2008) Responding to the linguistic reality of mainstream classrooms: Preparing all teachers to teach English language learners. In M. Cochran-Smith, S. Feiman-Nemser and J. McIntyre (eds) *Handbook of Research on Teacher Education* (3rd edn, pp. 606–636). Mahwah, NJ: Erlbaum.
Machelli, N. and Keiser, D. (eds) (2005) *Teacher Education for Democracy and Social Justice*. New York: Routledge.
Mahan, J. (1982) Native Americans as teacher trainers: Anatomy and outcomes of a cultural immersion project. *Journal of Educational Equity and Leadership* 2 (2), 100–109.
Marx, S. (2006) *Revealing the Invisible: Confronting Passive Racism in Teacher Education*. New York: Routledge.

McDonald, M. (2005) The integration of social justice in teacher education: Dimensions of prospective teachers opportunities to learn. *Journal of Teacher Education* 56 (5), 418–435.

McDonald, M. and Zeichner, K. (2009) Social justice teacher education. In W. Ayers, T. Quinn, and D. Stovall (eds) *Handbook of Social Justice in Education*. New York: Routledge.

Michelli, N. and Keiser, D. (2005) *Teacher Education for Democracy and Social Justice*. New York: Routledge.

Montecinos, C. (2004) Paradoxes in multicultural teacher education research: Students of color positioned as objects while ignored as subjects. *International Journal of Qualitative Studies in Education* 17 (2), 167–181.

Moule, J. (2005) Implementing a social justice perspective: Invisible burden for faculty of color. *Teacher Education Quarterly* 32 (4), 23–42.

Peske, H.G. and Haycock, K. (2006) *Teaching Inequality: How Poor and Minority Students are Shortchanged on Teacher Quality*. Washington, DC: Education Trust.

Reimers, F. (1994) Education and structural adjustment in Latin America and sub-Saharan Africa. *International Journal of Educational Development* 14, 119–129.

Robertson, S. (2008) Remaking the world: Neoliberalism and the transformation of education and teachers' labor. In M. Compton and L. Weiner (eds) *The Global Assault on Teaching, Teachers and Their Unions* (pp. 11–36). New York: Palgrave Macmillan.

Rodgers, C. (2006) The turning of one's soul – Learning to teach for social justice: The Putney Graduate School of Education (1950–1964). *Teachers College Record* 108 (7), 1266–1295.

Samoff, J. (1999) Institutionalizing international influence: The context for educational reform in Africa. In M. Samuel, J. Perumal, R. Dhunpath, J. Jansen, and K. Lewin (eds) *International Trends in Teacher Education* (pp. 5–35). Durban, South Africa: University of Durban-Westville, Faculty of Education.

Seidl, B. and Friend, G. (2002) Leaving authority at the door: Equal-status community-based experiences and the preparation of teachers for diverse classrooms. *Teaching and Teacher Education* 18, 421–433.

Sirotnik, K. (ed.) (2001) *Holding Accountability Accountable: What Ought to Matter in Public Education*. New York: Teachers College Press.

Sleeter, C. (2001) Preparing teachers for culturally diverse schools: Research and the overwhelming presence of whiteness. *Journal of Teacher Education* 52 (2), 94–106.

Sleeter, C.E. (2008) Equity, democracy, and neoliberal assaults on teacher education. *Teaching and Teacher Education* 8, 1947–1957.

Solomon, R.P. and Sekayi, D.N.R. (eds) (2007) *Urban Teacher Education and Teaching: Innovative Practices for Diversity and Social Justice*. Mahwah, NJ: Erlbaum/Routledge.

Tatto, T. (2006) Education reform and the global regulation of teachers' education, development and work. *International Journal of Educational Research* 45, 231–241.

Torres, R.M. (2000) From agents of reform to subjects of change: The teaching crossroads in Latin America. *Prospects* 30 (2), 255–273.

UNESCO (1998) *World Education Report*. Paris: UNESCO Publishing.

Vavrus, M. (2002) *Transforming the multicultural education of teachers*. New York: Teachers College Press.

Villegas, A.M. and Davis, D.E. (2008) Preparing teachers of color to confront racial/ethnic disparities in educational outcomes. In M. Cochran-Smith, S. Feiman-Nemser and D.J. McIntryre (eds) *Handbook of Research on Teacher Education* (3rd edn, pp. 583–605). New York: Routledge.

Villegas, A.M. and Lucas, T. (2002) Preparing culturally responsive teachers: Rethinking the curriculum. *Journal of Teacher Education* 53 (1), 20–32.

Villegas, A.M. and Lucas, T. (2004) Diversifying the teacher workforce: A retrospective and prospective analysis. In M. Smylie and D. Miretzky (eds) *Developing the Teacher Workforce* (pp. 70–104). Chicago: University of Chicago Press.

Villegas Reimers, E. and Reimers, F. (1996) Where are 60 million teachers? *Prospects* 26 (3), 469–492.

Walsh, K. (2004) A candidate-centered model for teacher preparation and licensure. In F. Hess, A. Rotherham and K. Walsh (eds) *A Qualified Teacher in Every Classroom* (pp. 223–254). Cambridge MA: Harvard Education Press.

Weiner, L. (2007) A lethal threat to teacher education. *Journal of Teacher Education* 58 (4), 274–286.

Zeichner, K. (1995) Reflections of a teacher educator working for social change. In F. Korthagen and T. Russell (eds) *Teachers Who Teach Teachers: Reflections on Teacher Education* (pp. 11–24). London: Falmer Press.

Zeichner, K. (1996) Educating teachers for cultural diversity. In K. Zeichner, S. Melnick and M.L. Gomez (eds) *Currents of Reform in Preservice Teacher Education* (pp. 133–175). New York: Teachers College Press.

Zeichner, K. (2003) The adequacies and inadequacies of three current strategies to recruit, prepare, and retain the best teachers for all students. *Teachers College Record* 105 (3), 490–515.

Zeichner, K. (2006) Reflections of a university-based teacher educator on the future of college and university-based teacher education. *Journal of Teacher Education* 57 (3), 326–340.

Zeichner, K. (2009) *Teacher Education and the Struggle for Social Justice*. New York: Routledge.

Zeichner, K. (2010) Rethinking the connections between campus courses and field experiences in university-based teacher education. *Journal of Teacher Education* 89 (11), 89–99.

Zeichner, K. and Melnick, S. (1996) The role of community experiences in preparing teachers for cultural diversity. In K. Zeichner, S. Melnick and M.L. Gomez (eds) *Currents of Reform in Preservice Teacher Education* (pp. 176–198). New York: Teachers College Press.

Chapter 2

Multimodality, Social Justice and Becoming a 'Really South African' Democracy: Case Studies from Language Classrooms

DENISE NEWFIELD

Fifty years after the birth of Bantu Education and 15 years after the demise of apartheid and the inception of a new unitary education system, the scourge of apartheid education remains. In spite of millions of rands having been poured into education since 1994 to support a radically new and progressive curriculum based on the principles of South Africa's newly democratic Constitution of 1996, South African education remains in a state of crisis. Near the bottom of international tables of literacy and numeracy achievement, even after ongoing curricular revisions and numerous teacher training initiatives and skills interventions, South African education is acknowledged as being in a mess, or, more strongly, as being a 'national disaster', the result of a 'toxic mix' of causes that come together to keep it in a state of 'disrepair' (Bloch, 2009). The question of social justice is currently backgrounded in the public domain and media amidst the panic around low skills, even though it is enshrined, as a philosophical and political principle, in the current South African curriculum.

This chapter focuses on the work of South African language teacher educators who attempt to work with past and present divisions in South African education – social, economic, material and academic (Newfield, 2009; Newfield *et al.*, 2003; Stein, 2003, 2008; Stein & Newfield, 2004). Our work in language, literacy and literature classrooms in universities and schools tries to integrate social justice education with the development of skills, sound teaching methodology and subject content knowledge. Our pedagogic practice seeks to undo narrow, authoritarian models of teaching and to reframe pedagogic assumptions. It situates teaching and learning in the multilayered contexts of contemporary South African life and attempts to promote transformation. The form of teacher education exemplified seeks to simultaneously 'undo' previous practices (Butler, 2004) and implement new ones. It seeks to fashion a new habitus (Bourdieu, 1994) in South African teachers and students that will enable them to be usefully literate and to participate in the processes of democracy, thus leading to productive personal, public and working lives (New London Group, 2000).

Unlike many of South Africa's post-1994 education policy documents – which are couched in abstract, decontextualized discourse, leading to a lack of understanding and buy-in by teachers – the focal educational projects of this chapter are concrete and embedded in specific classroom activities. They demonstrate a pedagogy founded on both criticality and creativity.

The chapter contextualizes our work as language educators within the context of South Africa's educational history and within conceptions and practices of social justice teacher education at the University of the Witwatersrand (Wits), Johannesburg, South Africa, at the present time. The body of the chapter describes three of our interventions. These are built upon frameworks of multiliteracies (New London Group, 1996, 2000) and multimodal social semiotics (Hodge & Kress, 1988; Jewitt & Kress, 2003; Kress, 1997, 2009; Kress & van Leeuwen, 2001). They take place in mother tongue and second language contexts and address a range of issues relevant to social justice language teacher education in South Africa at the present time, including the questions of representational resources, multilingualism and semiotic disempowerment/reempowerment. The conclusion to the chapter sums up the potential of teacher education and classroom practices and activities based on multiliteracies and multimodal social semiotics in relation to social justice education.

The South African Educational Context

The educational philosophy of South Africa's National Party government was segregationist and discriminatory, as is well known: 'We want no mixing of languages, no mixing of cultures, no mixing of races' (cited in Christie, 1991: 174). Different education systems were provided for the different race groups constructed in terms of its apartheid ideology: Christian National Education for white children and Bantu Education for black children:

> There is no place for [the Bantu] in the European community above the level of certain forms of labour. ... For that reason it is of no avail

to him to receive a training ... Until now, he has been subjected to a school system which drew him away from his own community and misled him by showing him the green pastures of European society in which he was not allowed to graze. (HF Verwoerd, Minister of Native Affairs, 1953, quoted in Rose & Tunmer, 1975: 266)

Apartheid education, with its 19 education departments, uneven distribution of human and material resources and separate curricula and examinations, was firmly in place from 1953 until 1994. The new African National Congress (ANC) government made a massive, well-motivated and generously funded attempt to overthrow apartheid education in favor of a unitary system based on principles of redress, equity, democracy and human rights. Its postliberation curriculum reveals a transformative curriculum policy, founded upon South Africa's new Constitution:

> The Constitution of the Republic of South Africa (Act 108 of 1996) provides the basis for curriculum transformation and development in South Africa. The Preamble to the Constitution states that the aims of the Constitution are to
>
> - heal the divisions of the past and establish a society based on democratic values, social justice and human rights;
> - improve the quality of life of all citizens and free the potential of each person;
> - lay the foundations for a democratic and open society in which government is based on the will of the people and every citizen is equally protected by law; and
> - build a united and democratic South Africa able to take its rightful place as a sovereign state in the family of nations.
>
> Education and the curriculum have an important role to play in realising these aims. The curriculum aims to develop the full potential of each learner as a citizen of a democratic South Africa. (Department of Education, 2002: 1)

The revised, postapartheid curriculum statement sets out a list of learner outcomes based on knowledge, skills and values that aim at creating 'an awareness of the relationship between social justice, human rights, a healthy environment and inclusivity'. Learners are encouraged to 'develop knowledge and understanding of the rich diversity of this country, including the cultural, religious and ethnic components of this diversity' (Department of Education, 2002: 2).

New identities, intended to contribute to the building of a new South African nation, are envisaged for teachers and learners. They should be constructed on the foundations of agency and independence, multi-skilled competencies, respect and equity. Post-1994 learners are urged to realize that

> [t]he promotion of values is important not only for the sake of personal development, but also to ensure that a national South African identity is built on values very different from those that underpinned apartheid education. The kind of learner that is envisaged is one who will be inspired by these values, and who will act in the interests of a society based on respect for democracy, equality, human dignity, life and social justice. The curriculum seeks to create a lifelong learner who is confident and independent, literate, numerate, multi-skilled, compassionate, with a respect for the environment and the ability to participate in society as a critical and active citizen. (Department of Education, 2002: 3)

Social Justice Teacher Education at Wits: Education for Democracy

The University of the Witwatersrand (Wits) in Johannesburg, South Africa, is one of the country's leading higher educational institutions. It is recognized as having been an 'open' and oppositional university under apartheid, even though it is now felt that the opposition did not go far enough. It is, like other educational institutions, seeking to transform itself into a South African or African as opposed to Eurocentric institution. Wits offers a range of educational qualifications – an initial four-year program for teaching at foundation, primary and secondary school levels; a postgraduate certificate in education that specializes in the training of teachers at senior secondary school levels; graduate courses in education and in particular school subject areas; and professional certificates that aim to upgrade the knowledge and skills of practicing teachers who are underqualified or who wish to improve their competence in particular areas of the curriculum.

Social justice teacher education in South Africa has specific challenges concerning class, race, religion, gender, disability and illness in light of its particular segregationist and discriminatory history. While the media currently paint a bleak picture of educational transformation at this point, social justice, as a notion, is uppermost in many teacher educators' minds, as attested to through interviews of teacher educators at our institutions that we have recently conducted.

Social justice education in South Africa may be summed up as 'education for democracy through democracy' (Linington, Interview, 8 September 2009). It is a form of citizenship education founded on human rights and which addresses in productive ways the diversity of South African society and classrooms (Ferguson, Interview, 1 September 2009). It involves assisting teachers to understand the social context in which they work and to exercise their agency in relation to the conditions under which children are living and learning. Mary Metcalfe, former Dean of the Wits School of Education and present Director-General of Higher Education in the ANC government, states that teachers must be encouraged to 'understand that their classroom exists in a social context – that they're not islands' (Interview, 30 August 2009). They must, she says, be prepared to think critically and to challenge authority where necessary; however, this can only be achieved through a deep understanding of inequity as it previously existed in apartheid education and as it continues to exist in spite of South Africa's current egalitarian policies. Since South African student teachers come from very different contexts and backgrounds, an important challenge for teacher educators, she says, is to help elite students to unpack their 'knapsack of privilege', in the words of McIntosh (1988), and, similarly, to help the disadvantaged to see the other side. In this way, both groups become conscious of how they fit into the broader context.

Although social justice teacher education necessitates an understanding of South Africa's educational history, it should not simply dwell on the evils of apartheid, according to Wits teacher educators. They are adamant that student teachers must work out what their *current* challenges are and become aware of the inequities and injustices of their own time. Alluding to Franz Fanon, Metcalfe states that 'every generation must find its own revolution'. To find their revolution, South African teachers need to move beyond an appreciation of the past and its legacies of inequity and inequality:

> ... you see it's more than that. It's really about being fully South African. It's quite scary to me how people live in such ignorance of other components of society. It's quite sad ... it's an orientation to life, to the country, and to be fair, most people living in the suburbs just don't really have enough opportunity to go beyond ... those opportunities have to be consciously sought. ... Teachers need to become *fully South African*. (Metcalfe, Interview, 30 August 2009)

Metcalfe focuses here on what she sees as a key project in social justice teacher education in postapartheid South Africa: that of the reinvention of identity in relation to society as a complex and diverse whole. This project involves reimagining who we are as teachers and where our responsibilities lie in relation to ourselves and others.

Lee Rusznyak's conceptualization of practice teaching in South Africa may be seen as an implementation of this view. For her, practice teaching in present-day South Africa should be an act of border crossing in which students are exposed to a range of contexts, learning environments and management systems. To this end, she arranges that groups of students from Wits teach in schools in townships and informal settlements and that urban students are posted to rural farm schools (Interview, 1 September 2009).

In contradistinction to the authoritarian and teacher-centered pedagogies of apartheid education, participatory pedagogies built on discussion, debate and negotiation are seen as essential to democratic educational practice. However, the relationship between language and social justice is an uneasy one in South Africa. 'Do we deny people the right to quality education because they can't speak English properly?' asks Ferguson (Ferguson, Interview, 1 September 2009). If English, and more especially written English, becomes the language of teaching, learning and assessment, then non-mother tongue teachers and learners are at a distinct disadvantage, says Linington. As she sums up the situation, 'Language, the *carrier* of understanding becomes the *barrier* to understanding' (Interview, 8 September 2009).

The Question of Social Justice in Language Teacher Education

South Africa has always been, and remains, a multilingual country. The recognition of 11 South African languages – Sepedi, Sesotho, Setswana, siSwati, Tshivenda, Xitstonga, Afrikaans, English, isiNdebele, isiXhosa and isiZulu – is a cornerstone of the New Constitution and of post-1994 educational policy. The constitution acknowledges and wishes to redress the 'historically diminished' use and status of the indigenous languages of its people, advocating that the state 'take practical measures to elevate the status and advance the use of these languages' (The Constitution of the Republic of South Africa, No 108 for 1996, p. 4). The Pan South African Language Board must promote the development and use of all official languages, other indigenous languages such as Khoi and San, sign language and languages used by the full range of communities and religions of South Africa's citizens (The Constitution of the Republic of

South Africa, 1996: 4–5). In educational institutions, the medium of instruction is a matter of choice. At the school level, the governing body of a school is responsible for deciding which should be the language of learning; at the tertiary level, the institution's executive makes the choice.

The post-1994 scenario is in many ways a complete transformation of the earlier status quo where language issues were firmly prescribed and circumscribed. Racial segregation was complemented by linguistic segregation during the apartheid period – there were schools for black and white children, but also for isiZulu speakers, isiXhosa speakers and English and Afrikaans speakers. The imposition of Afrikaans (the language of the descendents of the Dutch settlers) on black school children was seen as a form of oppression, of 'symbolic violence' (Bourdieu, 1994), and led directly to the student uprisings of 1976.

An ironic and unintended consequence of the policy of linguistic plurality and equity is that English has flourished as never before in the years since 1994, both in the public sphere more generally and in education specifically. Most educational institutions today opt for English as the language of teaching and learning, because they see it as providing *access* to the local and international marketplace, as being the key to success. This has given rise to the deeply problematic situation, both ideologically and pedagogically, in which the majority of South Africa's students in school and in tertiary education study in a language that is not their mother tongue. Similarly, they are taught by teachers whose mother tongue is not English but instead one of South Africa's indigenous languages and whose competence in English may therefore be lacking.

New literacy studies (Heath, 1983; Street, 1984) is interested in the different literacy practices of communities and the way these relate, or fail to relate, to the dominant practices in schools, or in other words, in the relationship between literacy practices and power. Street (1984) argues that literacy is not autonomous and neutral but implicated in power. Certain literacy practices are valued and privileged to the expense of others. In terms of social justice teacher education, a question arises concerning the hegemonic nature of certain literacy practices. Should not they be challenged so that all literacy practices may be equally valued? Why should it be an educator's role to ensure that the dominant practice is taught and thus perpetuated? On the other hand, certain literacies hold sway and are socially valued and educators need to teach these. Janks's (2004, 2009) conception of the 'access paradox' shows how giving people access to the dominant literacy practice ensures continued dominance of that practice. On the other hand, if one denies people access, they are marginalized.

A Multimodal Approach to Social Justice Language Teacher Education

The related frameworks of multiliteracies (New London Group, 1996, 2000) and multimodal social semiotics (Hodge & Kress, 1988; Jewitt & Kress, 2003; Kress, 1997, 2003, 2009; Kress *et al.*, 2005; Kress & van Leeuwen, 2001) underpin the work of Stein and Newfield that forms the core of this chapter. These frameworks tackle the question of linguistic hegemony, of language per se – as opposed to the hegemony of particular languages – on the basis of the repertoires for meaning-making, representation and communication that exist in all cultures and societies and that are growing exponentially in relation to technological advances. Language is thus seen as one *mode* among others. It is a crucial mode, but one that is being supplemented and challenged by, for example, the increasingly powerful usage of visual modes.

Both frameworks are founded on notions of justice, democracy and equity in society and in education. Multiliteracies argue for a literacy education that is plural in terms of both culture and representational practices. There is not one literacy, but rather many literacies. Multiliteracies is premised upon the existence of local and global literacies and their interconnectedness in today's world. It sees the strengthening of both as the aim of literacy education. The skill of 'negotiating difference' – cultural, social, linguistic and semiotic – is a major educational goal for multiliteracies. Developing this skill is seen as 'the only hope for averting the catastrophic conflicts about identities and spaces that now seem ever-ready to flare up' in the world (New London Group, 2000: 14).

Multimodal social semiotics approaches issues of diversity and democracy through a semiotic route; that is, it holds that a socially just education should take account of the range of meaning-making possibilities and scenarios that exist in the current communicational landscape and in the communities of learners. To focus on language only – and particular languages at that – in the face of the prominence of the visual and hybrid forms of communication that are prevalent in today's global, technologized world as they are in local and indigenous contexts including classrooms – is to be both out of date and out of touch with the meaning-making resources of learners.

Multiple forms of meaning-making, representation and communication – visual, auditory, bodily, linguistic and all these combined – thus form the foundation of a semiotics that is strongly grounded in the social. These resources for meaning-making, always culturally, socially and historically situated, offer multiple possibilities of semiotic production both in and out of schools and classrooms. Semiotic production is designed and orchestrated in terms of the 'interest' of meaning-makers: what they wish to articulate in a specific context. Meaning-making is considered to be agentive and innovative as well as situated. Multimodal social semiotics reconceptualizes language as one mode among a range of others – the visual, sonic, gestural, performative and so on – used in cultural practices worldwide, the contemporary media and the teaching and learning that takes place in classrooms. The theory dovetails with anthropological studies of Africa that demonstrate the multimodal character of African cultural production, its 'mix n match' and combinatorial quality of bricolage (Coplan, 2008; Finnegan, 2002, 2007). As a methodology, multimodal social semiotics provides tools for analyzing what goes on in classrooms, which is more than its language interactions (Kress *et al.*, 2005), and for analyzing teacher and student texts (Bhattacharya *et al.*, 2007; Newfield, 2009; Stein, 2008). As a pedagogy, it has encouraged complex, creative and varied practices of text-making in classrooms that are counter-hegemonic at the same time as supportive of traditional language development goals, as will be demonstrated in this chapter.

The work of Stein and Newfield in language, literacy and literature education in South Africa (Newfield, 2009; Newfield *et al.*, 2003; Stein, 2003, 2008; Stein & Newfield, 2004) informs teacher education at preservice, in-service and graduate levels. Operating in teacher education institutions and school classrooms, it serves teachers, curriculum and materials designers, and policymakers. The work brings together multimodal textual practice and social justice education. What students make to capture their meanings is given credence and value. The question of textual practice is placed within a human rights framework: democratic education should not outlaw, or ignore, the resources of students and their communities for learning and representation. Semiotic freedom is a human right (Stein, 2008).

The work of Stein and Newfield also tackles the 'access paradox' in language teaching and learning. It simultaneously challenges hegemonic language and pedagogic practices, valorizes cultural, epistemological and semiotic alterity *and* provides access to dominant language practices, as will be described later in the chapter. This work is offered here as an instance of social justice language teacher education in South Africa both during a time of repression and in the postliberation moment, a time of transition.

Case Studies of Social Justice Language Education in South African Classrooms

Three case studies of social justice language teacher education – operating within the frameworks of multiliteracies and multimodality – will now be outlined. Key features will be identified and described. The examples are situated, respectively, in an English teacher education classroom at Wits during the last decade of apartheid teacher education, in a foundation-level literacy classroom in a deprived area and in a high school literature classroom in the postliberation era.

The Enchanted Island

The first account analyses a text produced by preservice teachers for the teaching and learning of Shakespeare during the period 1977–1993, a period of segregated schooling and teacher education. Lecturers in the English Methodology course accepted as a given, though not uncritically, Shakespeare's position at the core of the secondary school language curriculum. They were intent on providing access for secondary school students to Shakespeare's plays in the face of their linguistic challenges through making Shakespeare relevant to South African and African concerns. In terms of social justice teacher education, they further intended to use Shakespeare's plays as a means of interrogating the apartheid regime. To these ends, they developed a Shakespeare dramatization activity that drew on reader response theory (Rosenblatt, 1970) and adapted Brown's 'free Shakespeare' approach to the teaching and learning of Shakespeare (Brown, 1974).

The preservice teachers were asked to participate in this pedagogic activity – to experience it themselves – so that they could use it in the schools, aware of its possibilities and pitfalls. An aspect or section of a play was 'freely' dramatized rather than strictly adhered to. Students were encouraged to see the play through a South African lens and to recast the Shakespeare play as they saw fit in order to convey their interpretation of it. The text could be modernized and indigenized. Students would study the text on their own, decide on the aspect they wished to examine and devise a means of presenting it in dramatic form to an audience consisting of their classmates, lecturers and other interested members of the Wits academic community.

One of the most striking productions was *The Enchanted Island*, a type of 'masked performance' produced by a group of 15 students in 1986 during the second 'State of Emergency' imposed by the nationalist regime in an attempt to quell political unrest. The 1980s were a time of intense political activity in South Africa – of increasing polarization. On the one hand, anti-apartheid activity was growing and strengthening – as evidenced, for example, in the 'rolling mass action' of the United Democratic Front, a newly constituted umbrella movement to take the liberation struggle forward while the ANC, Pan Africanist Congress and Black Consciousness movements remained banned; and, on the other hand, the state responded with increasing militarization, surveillance and intimidation to what it saw as 'social unrest'. Military vehicles and personnel were a common sight on the campus where teachers were being trained in the prevailing atmosphere of campus surveillance and intimidation. Schooling was constrained by numerous dictates and prescriptions. Using the pedagogic space provided by the Shakespeare dramatization activity, the students employed Shakespeare's *The Tempest* to critique apartheid ideology; they also produced a new, context-specific interpretation of the play. This challenged and subverted the conventional view of the play encapsulated in the Arden edition they were using (Kermode, 1964).

I argue that the semiotic resources that the students recruited – masks and mime rather than language – enabled and shaped this interpretation of *The Tempest*. Caliban was presented not as savage and barbaric but as 'the native inhabitant of the island'. He wore a mask resplendent in the oranges and browns of the African earth. It was wide-eyed and vibrant, if somewhat vulnerable, but blended harmoniously with the plant life of the island. Seemingly inspired by, and designed in accordance with, traditional African masks used in ritual ceremonies (Newfield, 2009; Turner, 1982), Caliban was represented as 'a magical creature ... the native of the island', in the words of Ann-Marie, the student mask-maker (Figure 2.1). Although the traditional view of Prospero as man of culture and learning was retained, Prospero's mask was topped by a typical Western explorer's helmet to indicate his role as a colonialist. Alonso's mask was modeled on a press photograph of P.W. Botha (Figure 2.2), the then President of South Africa; the hybridization represented them both as illegitimate usurpers of power.

In relation to the literary criticism of the day, *The Enchanted Island* encapsulated an alternative representation of Shakespeare's *The Tempest* – in keeping with those interpretations emerging in alternative and postcolonial Shakespeare criticism (e.g. Drakakis, 1985; Orkin, 1987) but which were not yet widely known or taught in South African universities at the time. It engaged deeply with questions of social justice and power in South Africa and provided, in a trenchant and powerful form, a critique of the dominant ideology. The masked performance was

Figure 2.1 Caliban, 'native inhabitant of the island'

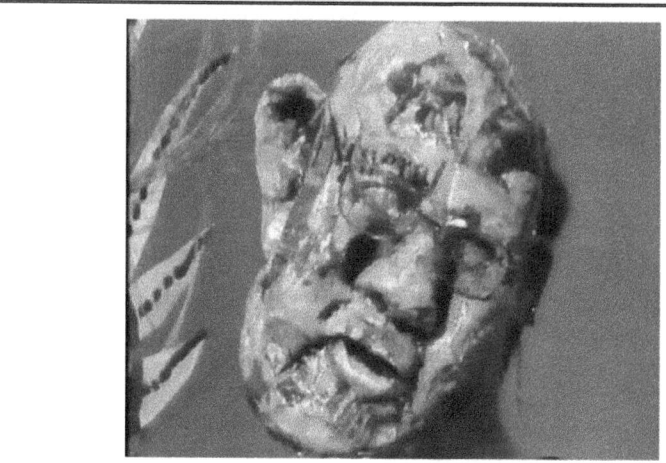

Figure 2.2 Alonso – P.W. Botha

a strategy of indigenization that enabled the white student teachers to critique colonialism, to align themselves with the plight of colonial subjects and, further, to reimagine themselves as Africans rather than as Europeans. This was an act of imaginative projection into a future, postapartheid South Africa.

The multimodal pedagogy created a space, in the face of a repressive and intimidatory political context, for learner teachers to 'own' their education and to talk back to the system and its canonical texts.

Language teacher education has too often been confined to the ivory tower as Zeichner suggests through his question: 'Where does the center of gravity lie, in the college or community?' (Zeichner, this volume: 14). The following two case studies are examples of language teacher education that originated not in the university but in poor communities and schools, where the teacher educators worked with practicing teachers at the coalface, exploring and researching alternative methods of teaching and learning in an attempt to lessen the scourge of Bantu Education in the decade after South Africa's liberation. Pippa Stein and I experimented with the application of the two emerging, linked frameworks for literacy education mentioned above – multiliteracies (New London Group, 2000) and multimodality (Kress, 1997, 2003) – in primary and secondary schools in 'townships' (ghettoes) outside Johannesburg. Our experiments gave rise to the Olifantsvlei–Manhattan Country School project and the Thebuwa Cloth project (Newfield *et al.*, 2003; Newfield & Maungedzo, 2006; Stein & Newfield, 2004).

A global multimodal exchange

Olifantsvlei Primary School is situated next to an informal settlement or 'squatter camp' on the outskirts of Johannesburg, where most of the children live in poverty and squalor. Tshidi Mamabolo and Ntsoake Senja, foundation level literacy and language teachers at the school, felt that their learners were passive, submissive and silent, and not engaging in meaningful communication in the classroom. One of the problems was the choice of English as medium of instruction, a choice made by the governing body of the school. Lessons were conducted with vocabulary cards aimed at teaching the letters of the alphabet and then simple common words, which learners were asked to repeat and use in sentences.

Manhattan Country School is a primary school in Manhattan, New York City, serving middle class children. A foundation level class was being taught by Janice Movson. Stein and Newfield set up a transnational exchange project on the subject of neighborhoods between the two schools. The project's aims were, first, to provide a relevant and exciting context for young children's language and literacy development – both in the mother tongue and in English, where English was not the mother tongue, and, second, to put the South African and American children in contact with one another. (It must be stressed that the South African children, not to mention the school, were not 'wired' – an e-mail or a blog project was therefore out of the question.) This project was based partly on the concept of deliberative democracy of political philosopher Iris Young (1996, 1997) and of Wits colleagues Penny Enslin and Shirley Pendlebury (Enslin *et al.*, 2001). Deliberative democracy proposes models of participation through processes of rational debate and discussion in classrooms in order to enhance students' ability to argue a point in a rational and cogent way, to see and appreciate different points of view and to be tolerant and accepting of others. Stein and Newfield felt it important at Olifantsvlei to extend Young's model of talk and debate in classrooms to other communicative forms. Gee and others have shown that Western forms of critical debate privilege those who have been inducted into this form of discourse – who know the rules of the game – and exclude those who have not had access to it (Fairclough, 1989; Gee, 1996), a point acknowledged by South African educators. A multimodal framework would provide opportunities for young students at Olifantsvlei and in Manhattan to use a range of semiotic forms rather than the dominant linguistic form only, each one conveying a different semiotic shaping of reality. Moreover, comparing the two neighborhoods across physical, class and cultural differences would provide different perspectives on the social world and allow students to see themselves *'relationally'* (Stein & Newfield, 2004). In this way, the critical multi-perspectivity that is at the basis of democracy might be fostered.

In this particular project, children at each site were asked to make a mural of their neighborhoods and homes, including self-portraits, photographs and letters. Each one was then sent to the partnership school and examined and discussed by the recipients. The effects of the exchange proved to be illuminating. First, the exchange provided the children with an authentic communicative task through which to pose questions and get answers. Second, it enabled the expression of feelings, ideas and identity in a range of modes – images, photographs, drawings and language. Third, it broadened the scope of the world for the children beyond their immediate environment to another quite different set of circumstances. Fourth, it produced a new audience for each set of children, an audience from a quite different class, culture and physical location. This produced a heightened and clearer sense of self and also of the way self is constructed through the other's gaze. For example, the Manhattan Country children, on seeing a photograph of Chicco Thandanzani, a 13-year-old member of the Olifantsvlei class, the son of a priest, in his bishop's hat, remarked not primarily on the hat but

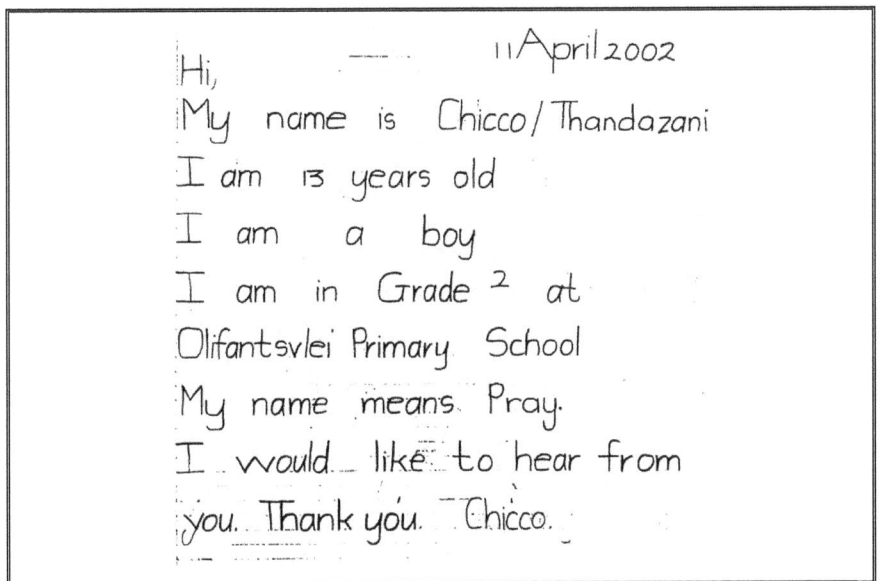

Figure 2.3 Chicco Thandazani's letter

on his age (Figure 2.3). 'What most fascinated our children is the fact that he is thirteen years old', wrote their teacher, Janice Movson (Stein & Newfield, 2004: 33). This provided an opportunity for the Manhattan children to discuss how it was that a boy of 13 years old had only recently started school. It led to more complex discussions around global inequality, the relationship between Africa and the West, the rich and the poor – important elements of social justice in the world from an African perspective. These discussions arose from a real situation rather than a textbook discussion of children's rights to education.

The Manhattan children remarked on the fact that the Olifantsvlei homes had toilets outside, while theirs were inside; the Olifantsvlei children said, 'I see you live in skyscrapers and I live in a shack' and 'I see that you speak English and I speak Zulu'. The materiality of the texts showed how the children made use of the different representational resources available to them. The Manhattan children cut up brightly colored paper to produce their apartment blocks with windows that could be opened to reveal photos of themselves and their families. The Olifantsvlei children produced fine pencil drawings on brown paper, with sand, leaves and grass stuck on (Figure 2.4).

Figure 2.4 Shack with toilet outside, pencil, crayon, paper and leaves stuck on

The researchers felt that the project was a first step in the direction of critical enquiry into global issues of social difference and social justice. In terms of this chapter, we feel that the project began to unpack the damage of apartheid education – its narrow provincialism, its prescribed forms of knowledge, its divisiveness – and to fashion instead a form of language and literacy learning more appropriate to the development of citizens fitted for democratic participation.

To speak: Poetry, performance and artifacts

The third case study is that of the Thebuwa Cloth project, which I undertook with teacher Robert Maungedzo in a poorly resourced secondary school in Soweto, in Robert's Grade 10 English Second Language classroom in 2002. As in the case of Olifantsvlei mentioned above, democracy had not brought the fruits of real learning to the formerly Bantu Education classrooms of the school, where practice was not in keeping with the vision and methods of the new post-1994 curriculum. The motivation for the Thebuwa project lay in this gap between policy and practice, ideology and achievement. Students in Robert's English classroom were reluctant to engage in the study of literature, even Southern African literature; their attitude to schooling was tainted by a disillusionment and cynicism with the value of education. As they put it, educated people were unemployed while criminals cruised the streets in luxurious automobiles. The initial aim of the project was to generate a spark of interest in literature, to motivate the students and, later, to encourage an appreciation of analysis and reflexivity, while stimulating reading, writing and cultural production more broadly. The researcher and teacher would take account of who the students were – their languages, semiotic resources, lifestyles, histories and epistemologies.

The project developed in a fluid, dynamic and democratic way in accordance with student responses and suggestions. It endured, unexpectedly, for over three years and beyond. It went through a number of phases or stages that may be described in two different ways: first, in terms of the learning activities and the texts produced by students; and second, in terms of its characterization by the teacher.

Most of the 55 students in Robert's Grade 10 English class were not reading their literature set books and did not even have copies of the books. Those who came to class – many played truant – expected notes to be dictated on the books' characters, plot and theme. Faced with this apathy and resistance, Denise Newfield, the teacher educator, and Robert Maungedzo, the teacher, decided to introduce the genre of poetry. Poetry had been dropped from the English curriculum at the school seven years previously on account of its supposed inaccessibility to students; but since poems could be photocopied, unlike novels, the literary text under examination could be handed out in class. It was hoped that a multimodal pedagogic approach might make some headway with students who were reluctant to use English. 'English suffocates my soul', one student had said; 'all this talk is strangling me', said another.

So began a transmodal program of drawing and sculpting the meaning of a poem and then writing a story about its issues; of researching and performing clan and family praise poems in indigenous African languages; of composing poems in English in which students portrayed their lives in Soweto; of writing letter-poems to one another (they did not have e-mail access or cell phones); of making a collective, multimodal artifact, later dubbed the *Thebuwa Cloth*; and of performing their own poems to one another at the start of English lessons.

Robert characterizes the project as a meaningful journey undertaken by himself in his role of teacher. Stuck in the 'station of reluctance', as he put it, he began a deep process of self-reflection. Trying out a new genre and pedagogy – with some skepticism – he moved to the 'station of uncertainty'. Journeying with the students through the varied terrain, at times determining the pathway and at other times following a path suggested by the students, he finally reached the 'station of agency',

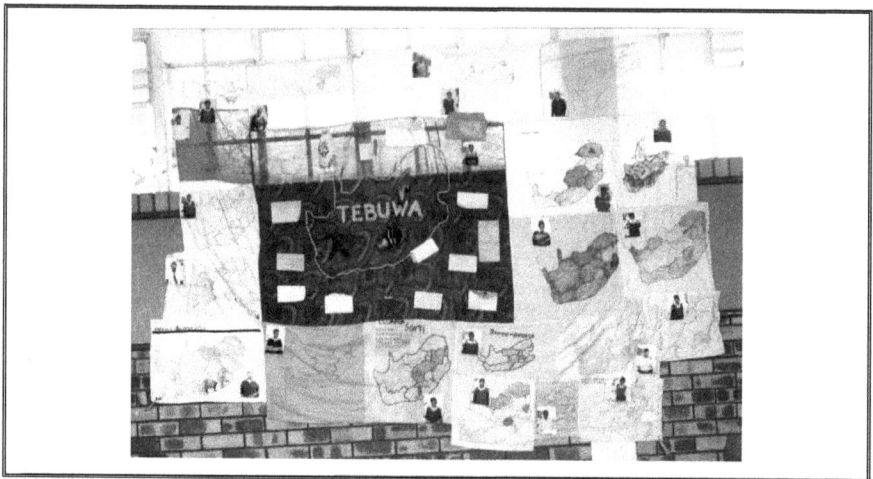

Figure 2.5 Thebuwa cloth

feeling more confident and empowered as a teacher of literature than before, newly energized by the level of participation of his students.

Figure 2.5 is a photograph of the Thebuwa Cloth that was sent as the students' 'ambassador' to China. It is 3.0 m by 2.8 m in size. It is constructed out of 22 smaller cloths made by individuals and groups, which have been stitched together. Motifs repeat themselves: embroidered maps of the new post-1994 geopolitical reconfiguration of South Africa; clan emblems; colored photographs of the students taken by a class member; praise poems in African languages painstakingly inked on the individual cloths; poems in English placed in recycled envelopes; dolls representing different ethnic groups placed around the central map.

The Thebuwa Cloth as a whole, in drawing on different semiotic resources and genres, Western and African, school-based and global, represented different facets of the students' identities – national, ethnic, clan, urban and personal. The materiality of the artifact itself was important. The choice of a collective cloth as the bearer of the students' message derives from Southern African cloth-making practices with which the learners were familiar, such as those of the Weya of Zimbabwe and the Minceka of the Limpopo Province in South Africa. The panel-like structure of the Thebuwa Cloth, the combination of visual and verbal forms of representation and the use of embroidery have a similar African provenance (Newfield, 2009; Schmahmann, 2000).

The name 'Thebuwa' was given to the cloth, and painted on it, after a lively class discussion. It means 'Speak' and is a coinage from 'to speak' in three of the different South African languages in the class ('thetha' in isiXhosa, 'bulabula' in Xitsonga and 'buwa' in Sepedi). Taken together, the cloth is a multimodal, heteroglossic artifact, portraying classroom identities in their diversity and commonality and in their multilayered forms – national, clan and ethnicity, youth, regional, and so on.

Two of the English poems enclosed in the envelopes represent key foci in the students' lives, their mothers (many are from single parent families) and the township itself, a place of vibrant life and hope, in their view. Their representations contrast strongly with earlier South African township poems by the generation of South African poets of the 1970s and 1980s, which protest against oppression and take a victim's stance.

Phillipine's 'The Best Mother Under the Sun' is constructed through a catalog of metaphors and similes:

> She is a mystery
> Like rain under water
> She can turn my life upside down
> Make fish to fly
> And birds to swim
> Reptiles to walk
> And mammals to crawl
> Turn predators into vegetarians
> And scavengers to be hunters.
> She is a queen in rags
> A sea without water
> An angel without wings
> A princess without a pony
> To be with her it's like Heaven to touch
> Angels to count
> And blue skies to taste.
>
> She is the queen
> Powerful like a scream
> One in a million
> Just like my favourite ice-cream.
> (Newfield & Maungedzo, 2005: 12)

Using the mother as a trope, Themba Kula's 'The Humble Soweto' depicts the township of Soweto, not as a mother unable to sustain her children (as in Mangane Serote's famous protest poem about Alexandra township in the 1970s) but as one filled with love, generosity and hope:

> The abbreviation is South Western Township
> The nickname, So, Where, To
> The foundation of talent and smiling faces
> People are not frowning like they smell faeces...
> Sowetans conquered pain
> They grew strong helped by the rain...
> Let's uplift Soweto's flame
> And not be afraid to aim.
> Our township is a resurrection
> We are still doing our correction
> It will soon be a perfection
> That will go with a mission
> We all have a bright vision
> They think Soweto is guilty
> But it's more like a city...
> Soweto is like the eyes of a child
> Who was killed for fun and pleasure
> During the uprisings
> But let us sing the songs of peace
>
> Hamba (Go), Soweto my love
> Hamba Sthandwa (Go my love)
> Mama of all the dark children.
> (Newfield & Maungedzo, 2005: 46)

Discussion

In outlining these projects from a perspective of social justice language teacher education, a number of features must be pointed out in their particular, South African-inflected implementations of multimodal and multiliteracies pedagogy. These are as follows:

(1) *The shift in power relations in the classroom* from top-down imposition to negotiation and discussion. This was an anti-hegemonic practice in the case study situated during apartheid but was in line with the democratic processes being emphasized in the postapartheid society and in the new educational policy. The prescriptive, discriminatory and punitive educational ethos, which tolerated and even encouraged corporal punishment, was giving way to a more critical,

learner-centered one. This created a pedagogic space that could nurture analytical and critical thinking in relation to power, context and identity, in which it was safe to explore and express alternative options for being and believing.

(2) *Expansion of the semiotic repertoire* of the classroom from language only to a range of modes, including the visual, actional, auditory and linguistic. Modes were selected for their appropriateness to particular representational and communicative purposes and carefully orchestrated into complex multimodal ensembles. This is highlighted in the Thebuwa Cloth project, where recycled maize bags became the material onto which emblems, maps and poems were painted, embroidered and inked. Production in one mode generated production in others, giving rise to ongoing creativity and semiotic production. Shifting meaning across modes enabled new ideas and interpretations and led to the reshaping of identity. The Olifantsvlei and Manhattan children were able to describe their neighborhoods through drawing and other visual forms in more complex ways than their limited competence in writing would have allowed. In Stein's terms, expansion of the semiotic repertoire, including in assessment tasks, from written language only to other forms is a 'right' of children in educational settings (2008).

(3) *Expansion of the linguistic repertoire* to include all the home languages of the students while retaining the emphasis on English as the target language. This was evident in the foundation-level classroom at Olifantsvlei and in the Thebuwa classroom. The resistance to English as an erstwhile language of the oppressor and as a language of authority and power was dispersed when the students' home languages were welcomed into the classroom. This allowed students to see English as a resource among many other linguistic resources. In the secondary school classroom, students composed in their mother tongues (praise poems) and in an English invigorated through local idiom and African languages (contemporary poems). So expressive and prolific were their poems that they were published in an anthology (Newfield & Maungedzo, 2005). I argue that the anthology testifies to the resolution of the 'access paradox' mentioned earlier (Janks, 2004, 2009). Establishing an atmosphere in a classroom where students and student teachers – especially second language speakers – feel comfortable to learn and experiment with language is a liberating experience and encourages second language acquisition. In a country where we have so many different language groups, multilingual language classroom practices encourage

teachers and students to appreciate other people's languages and cultures, to cease to fear them.

(4) *Incorporation of indigenous and local cultural and semiotic practices, histories and epistemologies into the classroom.* In the apartheid case study, white students used African ritual objects and masked ceremonies as inspiration for their representation of an alternative interpretation of Shakespeare's *The Tempest.* 'Hiding' behind the masks and using the body and its movements rather than the recognizable face and language facilitated a politically oppositional stance and a conception of self as African rather than Eurocentric. This practice broadened the approach to identity, interfacing home and community identities and histories with official South African curricular knowledge, which is derived from Western education systems.

As a genre, the Thebuwa Cloth has its provenance in southern African forms of cloth-making and came to serve as an identity object for the Soweto youth in the postapartheid moment. They were emboldened to reinvent themselves in relation to a brave new world. In using indigenous cultural practices for communicative purposes in the language classroom, the teaching students who used masks were able to confront and challenge the political regime; the young Olifantsvlei and Manhattan students were able to consider issues of poverty and affluence.

(5) *'Shifting the gaze' from the local to the global* (Stein & Newfield, 2004), *and putting the two into conversation.* Through this shift, the learners' imaginary horizon was expanded; they saw a range of realities and possibilities and this shifted their perceptions of self and their place in the world. This is highlighted in the exchange project between the Olifantsvlei and Manhattan children, as it is in the Thebuwa project, where the cloth traveled as the students' ambassador to China, and stimulated an exchange project with their peers at a school in the northern territories of Australia. Shifting the gaze enabled students to see the world from a range of perspectives, an essential component of democratic culture according to Young (1997). Zeichner (this volume) argues that teachers should be trained to teach in all contexts. At Wits, Rusznyak tries to achieve this through her approach to teaching practice in South Africa. In our language classrooms, Stein and I 'shifted our own gaze', that of the teachers and children with whom we worked in underresourced contexts and that of our student teachers, who examined and discussed the research studies in their courses.

These research studies have served as examples of how theory and practice can be integrated and of how the borders of class, ethnicity and race can be crossed. They demonstrate how both privileged and disadvantaged students can be taken on pedagogic journeys of discovery through 'breaking down the classroom walls and letting the world in', as Robert Maungedzo puts it.

Although not overtly or narrowly focused on questions of social justice, I argue that the above case studies are instances of social justice language teacher education. Foundational values of social justice education are dynamically interwoven with curricular skills and knowledge. Issues of social justice and democracy are not forced or contrived but emerge naturally and spontaneously from the basic principles of the theoretical framework supporting the pedagogy.

Conclusion

I have shown how the pedagogic approach in the language classrooms of this chapter brings about a convergence between the goals of language, literature and literacy education and those of social justice education. In the semiotically open classrooms I have described, young South Africans during apartheid and after have seized the opportunity to express themselves in multiple modes. Behind and through the masks, on and through paper and cloth murals, through movement, mime and oral performance, they have explored and etched their emergent and transforming identities. They have painted, drawn and made poems that speak powerfully of their aspirations, their views of history, of self in relation to others and to authority. They have traversed contexts of poverty and affluence. These young South Africans have taken steps to heal and to reimagine themselves and the nation. The case studies serve as examples of, and may be used as models for, a social justice language teacher education.

The challenge for us all is to acknowledge, encounter and accept the lifeworlds and experiences of others in our cosmopolitan, newly democratic state, to share ideas and expertise across historically and economically constructed boundaries, in order to narrow the educational gaps. For South African language teacher educators, the challenge is how to make language classrooms democratic spaces in which skills of creative thinking, criticality and articulation are put in the service of becoming 'fully South African' in the postapartheid moment.

However, what goes on in classrooms is not enough. Much more needs to be done to achieve 'quality and equality of education' (Isaacson,

2010) in a situation where some children live on rubbish dumps and go to school hungry and where some teachers remain in the shadows.

Acknowledgments

I am grateful to the teacher educators at the University of the Witwatersrand, who generously agreed to be interviewed on the subject of social justice teacher education during 2009 – Renee Ferguson, Vivien Linington, Leanne Rusznyak and Mary Metcalfe; also to students and graduates of Honors and Masters in English Education – Sindisiwe Murahwa, Rosemary Silverthorne, Tracy Workman-Davies and Katherine Naidu – for their participation in a focus group. I sincerely thank my research assistant, Sarah Key, for transcribing the interviews and for her helpful conversations. I continue to be inspired by the language teachers and learners whose classrooms are the sites of the case studies in this chapter and who opened up their hearts and minds to us – Tshidi Mamabolo, Ntsoake Senja and Robert Maungedzo. Finally, this chapter is a tribute to my research partner and friend, Pippa Stein, who passed away in 2007: Pippa, your legacy lives on.

References

Bhattacharya, R., Gupta, S., Jewitt, C., Newfield, D., Reed, Y. and Stein, P. (2007) The policy-praxis nexus in English classrooms in Delhi, Johannesburg and London: Teachers and the textual cycle. *TESOL Quarterly* 41 (3), 465–487.

Bloch, G. (2009) *Toxic Mix: What's Wrong with South Africa's Schools and How to Fix It*. Cape Town: Tafelberg.

Bourdieu, P. (1994) *Language and Symbolic Power* (J. Thompson, ed.; G. Raymond and M. Adamson, trans.). Oxford: Polity Press.

Brown, J.R. (1974) *Free Shakespeare*. London: Heinemann.

Butler, J. (2004) *Undoing Gender*. New York: Routledge.

Christie, P. (1991) *The Right to Learn: The Struggle for Education in South Africa* (2nd edn). Johannesburg: Ravan Press.

Coplan, D. (2007) *In Township Tonight: Three Centuries of South African Black City Music and Theatre* (2nd edn). Auckland Park: Jacana.

Department of Education (2002) *Revised National Curriculum Statement Grades R-9 (Schools), Languages*. Pretoria: Department of Education.

Drakakis, J. (ed) (1985) *Alternative Shakespeares*. London: Methuen.

Enslin, P., Pendelbury, S. and Tjattis, M. (2001) Deliberative democracy, diversity and the challenges of citizenship education. *Journal of Philosophy of Education* 35 (1), 115–130.

Fairclough, N. (1989) *Language and Power*. London: Longman.

Finnegan, R. (2002) *Communicating: The Multiple Modes of Human Interconnection*. London: Routledge.

Finnegan, R. (2007) *The Oral and Beyond: Doing Things with Words in Africa*. Oxford: James Currey.

Gee, J. (1996) *Social Linguistics and Literacies: Ideologies in Discourses* (2nd edn). London: Falmer Press.
Heath, S. (1983) *Ways with Words: Language, Life and Work in Communities and Classrooms.* Cambridge, UK: Cambridge University Press.
Hodge, R. and Kress, G. (1988) *Social Semiotics.* Cambridge, UK: Polity Press.
Isaacson, M. (2010) A plea to the literary consciences of our good ministers. *The Sunday Independent,* January 24, p. 17.
Janks, H. (2004) The access paradox. *English in Australia* 139, 33–42.
Janks, H. (2009) *Literacy and Power.* New York: Routledge.
Jewitt, C. and Kress, G. (2003) *Multimodal Literacy.* New York: Peter Lang.
Kermode, F. (ed.) (1964) *The Tempest* (The Arden Edition of the Works of William Shakespeare). London: Methuen, Arden Shakespeare Paperbacks.
Kress, G. (1997) *Before Writing – Rethinking the Paths to Literacy.* London: Routledge.
Kress, G. (2003) *Literacy in the New Media Age.* London: Routledge.
Kress, G. (2009) *Multimodality: A Social Semiotic Approach to Communication.* London: Routledge/Falmer.
Kress, G. and van Leeuwen, T. (2001) *Multimodal Discourse: The Modes and Media of Contemporary Communication.* London: Arnold.
Kress, G., Jewitt, C., Bourne J., Franks A., Hardcastle J., Jones K. and Reid E. (2005) *English in Urban Classrooms: A Multimodal Perspective on Teaching and Learning.* London: Routledge and Falmer.
McIntosh, P. (1988) *Unpacking the Invisible Knapsack.* Wellesley, MA: Wellesley College Center for Research on Women.
New London Group (1996) A pedagogy of multiliteracies: Designing social futures. *Harvard Educational Review* 66 (1), 60–92.
New London Group (2000) A pedagogy of multiliteracies: Designing social futures. In B. Cope and M. Kalantzis (eds) *Multiliteracies: Literacy Learning and the Design of Social Future* (pp. 9–37). London: Routledge.
Newfield, D. (2009) Transmodal semiosis in classrooms: Case studies from South Africa. PhD thesis, University of London.
Newfield, D., Andrew, D., Stein, P. and Maungedzo, R. (2003) No number can describe how good it was: Assessment issues in the multimodal classroom. *Assessment in Education* 10 (1), 61–82.
Newfield, D. and Maungedzo, R. (2005) *Thebuwa: Poems from Ndofaya.* Johannesburg: Denise Newfield Publications.
Newfield, D. and Maungedzo, R. (2006) Mobilising and modalising poetry in a Soweto classroom. *English Studies in Africa* 49 (1), 71–93.
Orkin, M. (1987) *Shakespeare against Apartheid.* Craighall: A. D. Donker (Pty) Ltd.
Rose, B. and Tunmer, R. (1975) *Documents in South African Education.* Johannesburg: A.D. Donker.
Rosenblatt, L. (1970) *Literature as Exploration.* London: Heinemann.
Schmahmann, B. (ed.) (2000) *Material Matters.* Johannesburg: Witwatersrand University Press.
Stein, P. (2003) The Olifantsvlei Fresh Stories Project: Multimodality, creativity and fixing in the Semiotic Chain. In C. Jewitt and G. Kress (eds) *Multimodal Literacy.* New York: Peter Lang.
Stein, P. (2008) *Multimodal Pedagogies in Diverse Classrooms: Representation, Rights and Resources.* London: Routledge.

Stein, P. and Newfield, D. (2004) Shifting the gaze in South African classrooms: New pedagogies, new publics, new democracies. *Thinking Classrooms* 5 (1), 28–36. Also published in *Peremina* 5 (1), January 2004. Vilnius, Lithuania: International Reading Association. On WWW at http://www.readingonline.org/international/inter_index.asp?HREF = /international/stein/ as Choice of the International Reading Association, November 2004.

Street, B. (1984) *Literacy in Theory and Practice*. Cambridge: Cambridge University Press.

The Constitution of the Republic of South Africa, Act 108 of 1996.

Turner, V. (1982) *From Ritual to Theatre: The Human Seriousness of Play*. New York: PAJ Publications.

Young, I. (1996) Communication and other: Beyond deliberative democracy. In S. Benhabib (ed.) *Democracy and Difference: Contesting the Boundaries of the Political*. Princeton: Princeton University Press.

Young, I. (1997) Difference as a resource for democratic communication. In J. Bohman and W. Rehg (eds) *Democracy: Essays on Reason and Politics*. Cambridge, MA: MIT Press.

Chapter 3
Does Intercultural Bilingual Education Open Spaces for Inclusion at Higher Education?

MAHIA MAURIAL and MOISÉS SUXO

Introduction

In the last few decades Intercultural Bilingual Education (IBE) has widely developed in Peru and Latin America. For the aim of developing this chapter, we focus on a Peruvian undergraduate experience of IBE that promotes access for Peruvian indigenous students; this is the Program of IBE at the University *Enrique Guzmán y Valle – La Cantuta*. This teachers' university is located in Lima, Peru. The Program (as we call it in this chapter) was initiated in year 2001, with the recovery of Peruvian democracy.

The aim of this chapter, while not an attempt to evaluate the Cantuta Program, is to emphasize some critical aspects that could be improved to emphasize Social Justice Teacher Education (SJTE). The Cantuta Program is a paradigmatic case where IBE Teaching Education is developed. This is because most of the Program students are indigenous and belong to indigenous villages.

We build this chapter as a product of our own experience with IBE Teacher Education. Our experience permits us to take notice of the shortages of the Cantuta Program, contrasting it with the PROEIB ANDES (IBE Program for the Andean countries in Cochabamba at the *Universidad Mayor de San Simón*). There Moisés Suxo was a student and Mahia Maurial a professor.[1] Also, the fact that Suxo was a professor of the Cantuta Program contributed to our ability to obtain evidence for understanding indigenous students' and nonindigenous students' relationships.

In this chapter we present the sociocultural context in Latin America to pinpoint the scope of practicing IBE with indigenous peoples as subjects. We continue defining IBE and summarize the historical process of its existence. We find commonalities between IBE and SJTE. We then present the IBE Program of *La Cantuta* and analyze some important aspects of the Program, i.e. learning methodology and issues of research. We present interculturality on the scope, and quoting students' voices (we introduce some testimonies of students that were recorded in year 2007, while Suxo was a professor at the IBE Program of *La Cantuta* (Suxo, in press)),[2] we focus on intercultural relationships between indigenous and nonindigenous students. Finally, we conclude that IBE, as it is practiced in Universidad La Cantuta, begins to build space for inclusion; we believe that interculturality is partially developed.

Latin American sociocultural context

Before defining what IBE is, it is important to contextualize the cultural, social and economic reality of Latin America. This region is a heterogeneous society with multiple socioeconomic inequalities. Around 10% of the total population of Latin America is formed by indigenous peoples (López & Küper, 2002) who speak indigenous languages, such as Mayas in Central America (particularly in Guatemala), Quechua and Aimara in the Andes of Peru and Bolivia, Guarani in the Chaco region of Bolivia, Paraguay and Argentina, and several Amazonian languages in Colombia, Brazil, Peru, Ecuador and Bolivia.

In some nation-states, indigenous populations form the majority of the countries' population, such as Bolivia and Guatemala. They are not minorities. In Peru, indigenous population represents over 40% of the national population (López & Küper, 2002). There exist 42 indigenous languages in Peru.

Historically, indigenous peoples have been oppressed in Latin America since the conquest by Spaniards of American-Indians five centuries ago. As a result of a long struggle, indigenous peoples are the poorest of the society. Illiteracy rates are concentrated among indigenous peoples (López & Küper, 2002). There are also limited resources among indigenous peoples for adequate health and nutrition.

Intercultural Bilingual Education

IBE is understood as a type of education that promotes indigenous cultures' revitalization, respects indigenous cultures and works to overcome cultural inequalities and conflict and to open a productive dialogue among cultures.

Following López (2003), IBE has its origins in the Arhuac area of the Black River in Venezuela, in 1974, when it was discussed in the frame of the Main Project of Education as an educational proposal targeted to indigenous populations.

During the 1940s and until the 1970s of the past century, education in Latin America targeted to indigenous populations was called bilingual education and considered as an education in indigenous language and Spanish. The intercultural aspect was not developed at that time. Around the 1970s and 1980s, the term bicultural referred to an education both in Western and indigenous culture. During the 1930s in Ecuador, Peru and Bolivia, there were personal teachers' initiatives in bilingual education; bilingual education was also developed by an evangelist institution, *Instituto Lingüístico de Verano*, since the 1940s. IBE was expanded later, during the 1970s and 1980s, among some universities with the support of international cooperation. Some examples are *Proyecto Experimental de Educación Bilingüe de Puno* with the *Universidad del Altiplano* in Peru or the IBE Project in Ecuador.

IBE was born with the aim to civilize the uncivilized, with a transitional model toward the learning of Spanish and Western culture. The model of 'development and maintenance' – of indigenous languages and cultures – has emerged during last three decades; however, in practice this model confronts a passive and colonialist educational system where the aim is still to civilize and to offer literacy in Spanish.

Nonetheless, IBE was absorbed during the 1990s and 2000s by indigenous movements and organizations as part of its liberation peoples' projects. This is the case, for example, of AIDESEP (*Asociación Interétnica de Desarrollo de la Selva Peruana*) in the Amazon Basin of Peru and CONAI in Ecuador.

It is important to mention that interculturality (meaning the promotion of dialogue among cultures) as a principle is opened to all students in Peru – indigenous, African American, *mestizo*[3] and white students – as it is sanctioned by the – in force – General Law of Education. To the contrary, IBE Teacher Education is opened to indigenous people as they are the ones who are members of indigenous cultures and who speak indigenous languages.

IBE and SJTE

Certainly, IBE possesses a strong social and political dimension. The aim of IBE is to build a more inclusive society that respects the multilingual and pluricultural reality of the Latin American nation-states. IBE is a multicultural and antiracist education that seeks equity and the practice of social justice education.

As indigenous peoples, indigenous languages and indigenous cultures in Latin America have been oppressed since the colonial era, to practice IBE is to support a decolonizatory discourse and practice and to affirm indigenous peoples' self-determination.

IBE Teacher Education has commonalities with SJTE, as both 'help to bring about broad scale social change in the social, economic, political, and educational spheres of society' (Zeichner, this volume: 10). IBE teachers are prepared to reconstruct schools toward a more inclusive curriculum and more inclusive learning and to reconstruct society toward social equity.

Another commonality of SJTE and IBE Teacher Education is that both 'shift the center of gravity of teacher education from the university campus to communities' (Zeichner, this volume: 14). Although the emphasis given to communities varies from IBE Program to Program, IBE focuses on indigenous language and knowledge that occurs as part of informal education within communities.

In this respect IBE has developed and practiced an agenda of community participation, or the involvement of wise men and wise women, parents, grandparents, and other relatives and members of the community in students' learning. For example, wise men and wise women give lessons in school classrooms and students visit craftsmen and craftswomen and other specialists in their houses or farmers in their farms. This agenda has also been brought into IBE Teacher Education Programs.

It is important to pinpoint that SJTE and IBE Teacher Education have also in common the claim to develop in prospective students a 'clearer sense of their own ethnic and cultural identities and their own social location and knowledge of how various forms of privilege operate in their society' (e.g. in Zeichner's context, white and English language privilege) (Zeichner, this volume: 15). Spanish language, which is the language of the marginalized Latino in the United States (immigrants), seems to be the privileged language in most parts of Latin America (with the exception of Portuguese in Brazil). In this way IBE Teacher Education goes deep in this privilege and studies, for example, forms of *diglossia*.

The IBE Program of *Universidad Nacional de Educación Enrique Guzmán y Valle – La Cantuta*

The undergraduate IBE Program of *Universidad Nacional de Educación Enrique Guzmán y Valle – La Cantuta* (a teachers' university) began in 2001 with the aim 'to contribute to studies and to critical analysis of country's general problem, particularly national education, considering multiculturality, poli-ethnicity and interculturality of our society' (Universidad Nacional de Educación Enrique Guzmán y Valle, cf. Rosales 2007: 77).

As associate professor of the Program, María Rosales narrates[4]:

> The Program was promoted by the professors of the College of Arts. The idea was born since the nineties and when Peruvian democracy was restored, in year 2001, the Program Act of Creation was obtained as part of the department of communications. The justification of the IBE Program was the consideration that the Teachers' University *La Cantuta* should have toward indigenous sectors of the country.

Rosales continues:

> To complete IBE teacher education we considered IBE Teacher Education for middle school ... When we organized the Program there were 10 Normal schools that educate IBE teachers for elementary schools only, and there were no IBE teachers for middle schools. IBE was cut off at this level. We believe that IBE should be offered at all levels due to the pluricultural nature of our country.

Thus, the Program prepares middle school (*secundaria* level in Peru) IBE indigenous teachers. To enter the Program, an important requirement is to be indigenous and speakers of indigenous languages. Indigenous students share general preparation with nonindigenous students of the university.

Indigenous students of the IBE Program and of different programs that the university offers find access to the Program through conventions among universities, boroughs and indigenous organizations. The main objective of the conventions is 'to improve the academic level of the best students of the villages'. The authorities of the villages select the best students to guarantee students' access to higher education.

Currently 223 students have finished their bachelor studies in the IBE Program and 41 students passed the exam or developed a thesis and possess a professional title in pedagogy (Rosales, 2009).

As students belong to impoverished families, both the university and indigenous organizations and boroughs support students' expenditures through scholarships, including students' fees and nurturance (use of the dining room) and ladies' rooms. María Rosales informs us that 'these benefits are given to students at the time they enter to university. If they keep good records, they maintain these benefits. The best students also obtain university jobs'.

Students are members of six ethnic groups, *Quechua, Aimara, Jacaru, Shipibo, Aguajun* and *Ashaninka*. Recently, African Peruvian students entered the Program. Most of these students were born in small rural indigenous villages, and they arrived in the capital city for the first time to study at the university.

Most students who finished studies returned to their villages because they possess a strong sense of membership (to their villages and to indigenous organizations) and willingness to work for peoples' development. This is an ideal that is articulated by a student during the time of studies: 'I will return to work to my village and to share what I have learned here at the university with the youngster of my village' (Dalila,[5] 25 years, Awajun) (Suxo, in press).

General teaching courses that IBE students share with every student at the university are General Psychology; Society, Culture and Education; Psychology of Development; Educational Theory; General Didactics; Educational Evaluation, Curriculum Theory; Orientation to Personal Development; Educational Projects; Ethics and Teachers' Deontology and Educational Management.

Core courses that are offered by the IBE Program are Andean Linguistics, Introduction to IBE, Phonetics of Native Language, Amazonian Linguistics, Native Language I, II and III, Native Literature Workshop, Phonology of Native Language, Syntax of Native Language, Teaching of Spanish as a Second Language, Native Language Literature Creation, Didactics of Native Languages Workshop, Development projects in IBE, Quechua Writing and Sociolinguistics Research Workshop. Students develop a major in IBE and a minor in Spanish Language and Literature.

As we can see the Program emphasizes language and literature and there is a lack of development of cultural content, as María Rosales (2007) pinpointed. There is also a lack of sociopolitical content, such as the analysis of indigenous social reality and history and analysis of indigenous movements in the country and in the South American region. Finally, the IBE Program is not articulated to content related to productive development of the environment contextualized to biodiversity conservation.

We can see that there is the need to reformulate the curriculum of the IBE Program in order to respond to indigenous peoples' demands. The reformulation of the curriculum should have the social participation of indigenous movements.

Learning methodology

In this section we discuss the importance – in IBE Teacher Education – of opening teaching and learning to oral tradition and cultural memories that students possess and to native methods of learning and teaching that have passed from generation to generation in students' cultures.

Indigenous hands-on ways of learning on the ground should be connected to academic ways of teaching and learning. Traditional academic ways of teaching such as expositions, use of blackboard, individual examinations, book readings and paper writing should be nurtured with native ways of teaching and learning such as storytelling. This kind of knowledge is not developed in the Program.

Among indigenous villages, learners are guided constantly by an adult who orients with 'the example'. Among these villages, wise men or wise women (*yachaq* in Quechua and *yatiri* in Aimara) are elders who inspire with their words the behavior of youngsters. Indigenous wise men or wise women are repositories of indigenous knowledge and indigenous ways of knowing. We believe that they should be invited to university forums.

It is also crucial to connect higher education learning to community[6] life. Indigenous socialization that is based on experiential learning, expressed in actions such as observation, practice, experimentation, imitation (for the Quechua case, see García, cf. Julca, 2007; for the Aimara case, see Suxo, 2005) should not be separated from academic learning.

An important advancement in methodology of the Program is cooperative learning. Cooperative learning is based on indigenous ways of human relationship that is *Ayni* (traditional collective reciprocal work of the Andean region).

Cooperative learning is practiced through team work that is enhanced by professors in two ways: (1) having teams composed of students of the same ethnic background; (2) having teams composed of students of different ethnic backgrounds. The first way is commonly used in indigenous linguistics. Cultural issues could be worked by the first or the second way, depending on the professor's objective.

María Rosales mentioned how cooperative learning is practiced in the Program:

> This way of working (cooperative learning) permits the best learning among all the courses, especially the ones that are of general formation. This learning permits indigenous students to organize groups by ethnic origin. Students discuss problems and needs in their indigenous languages. This is the first approximation to subjects

that are new; and later they work in Spanish, to be able to expound and present their work in the classroom, in front of every peer.

Treating problems and needs in indigenous languages gives confidence to students. Spanish is the *lingua franca* or the language understood by the whole group of students; this is why students expound to the class in Spanish after they work in groups in indigenous languages.

Here we have established some aspects that nurture the work of intercultural learning methodologies, which promote a dialogue between scientific and indigenous knowledge. At this point we introduce the issue of research that we believe is crucial for an academic program. It is important to identify some aspects for building an intercultural research practice, which promotes a dialogue between scientific and indigenous knowledge.

About research

To work on research based on IBE means to reorient research work conceiving different research logics that are embedded in indigenous worldviews and value systems. There exist diverse cultural logics; thus, there exist diverse research logics.

Following Tuhiwai Smith (2002), we believe that research is not in the domain of the experts 'with advanced qualifications of (formal) education' (p. 125). Research is in the domain of communities as the main actor of an agenda of explorations, understanding and action (Maurial, 2007).

Positivist school of thought has conceived of informants as objects of study. Nowadays it is clear for postmodern thinkers to conceive of persons who act on the research not as merely informants but as subjects of study, or in other words, as the actors of the research. This is particularly important in research targeted to indigenous peoples. In this way indigenous IBE students should be *catalyzers* of research.

We believe that collaborative research is the type of research that is congruent with this vision. Collaborative research searches for the transformation of reality (Schensul & Schensul, 1992).

As Schensul and Schensul affirm about collaborative research:

> First and foremost, collaborative research should be viewed as a tool for the empowerment of those groups within limited access to good data and the methods that produce such data. Populations that historically have had limited access to data and to quantitative research methods and results include women, ethnic minority groups, and the poor. Data enhance the ability of any group to understand its

target population, promote its own interests, attract new resources, and see itself and its constituencies in relation to others. (Schensul & Schensul, 1992: 195).

We believe that *La Cantuta* IBE Program should promote collaborative research.

Furthermore, while doing research with indigenous peoples, it is crucial to promote a dialogue among different types of knowledge. This means to open epistemological bridges among scientific knowledge – based in written academic sources, and indigenous knowledge – based in oral sources (Maurial, 2007). A dialogue among knowledges implies a social process of learning that occurs on the ground, in which plural worldviews and values of everyday life connect with values of academic origin.

The IBE Program is far away from the type of research that we defend above. We were informed that research at the IBE Program is only based on second source information. Cultural practices, social organization and socioeconomic situations of students' ethnic groups are the core of research. Although students create research projects, usually fieldwork is not completed.[7] We believe that university financial problems or lack of grants could explain the lack of fieldwork among students. Lack of fieldwork and lack of a congruent intercultural way of doing research impede students from developing a dialogue among knowledges while doing research.

Interculturality on the scope

Importance of interculturality in higher education

Although in Peru there are few higher education IBE Programs,[8] the impact of these Programs does not transcend the colonizatory logic of the university that follows the logic of formal education in general. While inextricably linked with the Progress Myth (or the belief of a straight line in human evolution), formal education keeps away the indigenous membership of indigenous people (*desindigenizar* in Spanish) (Depaz, 2005; Maurial, 1999; Monroe, 2006).

Thus, to develop interculturality at the university does not simply mean to give a course or some courses about interculturality; it is to change the colonizatory logic of university to one that celebrates diversity. This means to change discriminatory relationships among indigenous and nonindigenous students. As Ladson-Billings (cf. Zeichner, this volume: 16) affirms, one of the practices of SJTE – that is also one IBE practices – consists in 'incorporating a commitment to diversity in program and institutional contexts and not just in individual courses'.

Intercultural relationships among students of the IBE Program

As we see below, interculturality as a practice and an attitude flows by different paths in university life at the IBE Program, from a tense relationship at the beginning of the studies to the transit of mutual understanding at the end of the career. Each student, indigenous or nonindigenous, possesses a particular experience in coexistence with the 'other', who is different.

Relationships among students of the IBE Program began with the rediscovery of the other's existence in Lima, the capital of the country, where the presence of indigenous immigrants is a reality in the last five decades. The perception of students from Lima, sons and daughters of indigenous immigrants, is revealing:

> I have never seen closely these persons from the jungle, this means persons purely from communities. At the beginning I was surprised by their physical features and their speech. I know that they also looked at me closely, as I do. (Gabriela, 30 years, *mestiza*) (Suxo, in press)

Following we analyze some students' perceptions of interculturality as they experience and encounter it in their lives. Relationships are contradictorily qualified as 'positive', 'distant', 'indifferent' and with the presence of 'opposed values'. Through students' experience we visualize an interculturality under construction, a latent historical conflict from an indigenous view: 'They treat us well and some are aware that they admire because we speak the language that they use ... others treat us with scorn' (Juan, 24 years, Awajun) (Suxo, in press).

A distinctive feature is the opinion of a student from Lima: 'From what I have seen, relationships of the majority are not agreeable. Fellows feel discrimination from students from Lima who despise them. Even in some moments they have argued' (Rosa, 24 years, *mestiza*). Even as urban (there exists discrimination of urban population over rural population), she is more sensitive to indigenous culture than her peers from Lima; this is maybe why she has no problems in living with her boyfriend, a Quechua-speaking student.

Language is one of the subjects that causes conflict between indigenous and nonindigenous students, as an indigenous student affirms: 'Language is for them (nonindigenous students) a dialect that has no writing and therefore does not do a lot of good' (Eduardo, 29 years, Shipibo) (Suxo, in press). This situation is fueled by the fact that indigenous students do not express themselves as do native speakers of Spanish, their second language.

However, good relationships among students with different ethnic origins have improved in recent semesters as Kenny emphasizes: 'I am happy to give moral incentives to my fellows of the classroom because today they are not as before, when we were in first semester. They are different, thanks to them who are sharing with us (he refers to *mestizo* fellows)' (Kenny, Awajun) (Suxo, in press).

Professor María Rosales also emphasizes the improvement of good relationships:

> Relationships among students are warm. At the beginning (of the program) non-indigenous students treated indigenous students with certain commiseration, but after a time of cohabitation, treatment changed evidently. Indigenous students showed that their linguistic and cultural differences were 'a plus' that non-indigenous students began to value.

Mutual understanding is the result of the cohabitation, getting to know the 'other', the different one. Institutional contexts have changed, as Rosales pinpoints:

> They (indigenous students) are positioning progressively in university space, for example they carry out food exhibitions by regions and ethnic groups, they teach indigenous languages at the Students' Center to indigenous and non-indigenous peers and to professors and university workers, and they present dances and songs. Andean New Year's Eve celebration and solstice celebrations, following Andean calendar, have been institutionalized.

Following Ladson-Billings (cf. Zeichner, this volume), changes in institutional contexts express a commitment to diversity. These changes – although conflicts and contradictions are still present – have permitted students to begin to share cultural manifestations at least vaguely.

In conclusion, good intercultural relationships of university life seem to be improved; this means that interculturality is lived as a process under construction, i.e. to reach equity through diversity. In this context, it is possible to dream of an intercultural university in the wide sense of the term only if work with urban students is reinforced, as they are the most inclined to indolence in front of the reality of indigenous peoples.

An important point is: How will students' socialization impact their future practice as teachers? As with the initial discrimination of nonindigenous students against indigenous students, there seems to be a change toward a dialogue among 'different'; this could help future teachers to inculcate in their students a dialogue among different ethnic groups. However, this requires a previous space of individual and collective reflection – a metacognition – that should be part of IBE preparation.

Conclusions

At this point, we believe that IBE Teacher Education, as is practiced at the *Universidad La Cantuta*, opens little spaces for indigenous students' inclusion; interculturality is partially developed.

Through this chapter we see that actors of IBE Teacher Education practice SJTE in the way that IBE begins to be positioned in the university institutional context. In spite of initial discriminatory relationships of nonindigenous students toward indigenous students, we see an initial process of openness to dialogue and mutual understanding among students. Indigenous languages are practiced among courses and indigenous cultures begin to be present in institutional life. However, sociopolitical and cultural aspects of knowledge should be addressed through courses. Linguistics is important, but an interdisciplinary scenario could feed the curriculum.

Nonetheless, professors and students do not practice interculturality to the extent it could be practiced; this is evident in the way of learning (learning methods) and in the way of doing research (in spite of the practice of cooperative learning). Intercultural relationships between academic life and community life should be enhanced. A dialogue between indigenous and scientific knowledges could be born from these relationships.

Notes

1. Moisés Suxo, an indigenous *Aimara* teacher, was a student from 2004 to 2006 at the Master's Program of PROEIB Andes, IBE Program for the Andean countries in Cochabamba, at the *Universidad Mayor de San Simón*. Mahia Maurial was a professor at the same Program from 2002 to 2004. Moisés Suxo was later a professor at the undergraduate Program of IBE of *Universidad Enrique Guzmán y Valle – La Cantuta*, in Lima, in 2007.
2. While Suxo taught the course of Sociolinguistics Workshop, he developed a personal research project. For this project, he requested students to complete some information in the form of interviews. Later the voice of one of the Cantuta Program's founders was obtained by an interview in the context of this chapter writing.

3. A *mestizo* is a cultural category that emphasizes the mixture of cultures and mixture of races that a person possesses.
4. We appreciate the collaboration of María Rosales, professor of the IBE Program at *Universidad de Educación Enrique Guzmán y Valle – La Cantuta*, who was interviewed for the purpose of collecting data for this chapter.
5. All students are referred to by pseudonyms.
6. Among indigenous peoples, *community* (*Ayllu* in Quechua and Aimara) is the collective entity inherent to people's existence. It is more than a geographic unity as a village; people are reunited by ethnic, spiritual and historical dimensions and possess a common vision of the future.
7. Information given by Professor Rosales.
8. There exists the Program of *Universidad La Cantuta* in Lima, the Program of *Universidad Santiago Antúnez de Mayolo* in Ancash, the Program in *Universidad del Altiplano in* Puno and the Program in *Universidad Nacional Mayor de San Marcos* with ARPI in Satipo.

References

Depaz, Z. (2005) Nuestra pluriculturalidad y la tarea de repensar radicalmente el lugar de universidad en el Perú. In L. Tejada (ed.) *Los estudiantes indígenas amazónicos de la UNMSM*. Lima: Universidad Nacional Mayor de San Marcos.

Julca, F. (2007) Recursos humanos para la Educación Intercultural Bilingüe. In E. Vilchez, S. Valdez and M. Rosales (eds) *Interculturalidad y Bilingüismo en la Formación de Recursos Humanos: Educación, Medicina, Derecho y Etnodesarrollo*. Lima: CILA, Universidad Nacional Mayor de San Marcos, UNALM, UNE, PROEIB Andes, CAAAP.

López, L.E. (2003) La cuestión de la interculturalidad y la educación latinoamericana. In R. Sumalavia (ed.) *Ante el espejo trizado*. Lima: Universidad Católica.

López, L.E. and Küper, W. (2002) La Educación Intercultural Bilingüe en América Latina. Lima: GTZ.

Maurial, M. (1999) Indigenous knowledge and schooling: A continuum between conflict and dialogue. In J. Kincheloe and L. Semali (eds) *What Is Indigenous Knowledge? Voices from the Academy*. New York: Falmer Press.

Maurial, M. (2007) Algunas reflexiones sobre la formación de docentes e indígenas como investigadores. In E. Vilchez, S. Valdez and M. Rosales (eds) *Interculturalidad y Bilingüismo en la Formación de Recursos Humanos: Educación, Medicina, Derecho y Etnodesarrollo*. Lima: CILA, Universidad Nacional Mayor de San Marcos, UNALM, UNE, PROEIB Andes, CAAAP.

Monroe, J. (2006) Interculturalidad y formación superior: la subjetividad indígena en la modernidad reciente. In P. Díaz Romero (ed.) *Caminos para la inclusión en la educación superior*. Lima: OEI.

Rist, S., Zimmerman, A. and Wiesmann, U. (2004) From epistemic monoculture to cooperation between epistemic communities – Lessons learnt from development research. *Conference Bridging Scales and Epistemologies – Linking Local Knowledge and Global Science in Multi-Scale Assessment, Alexandria*.

Rosales, M. (2007) La educación intercultural bilingüe en la Universidad Nacional de Educación Enrique Guzmán y Valle. In E. Vilchez, S. Valdez, and M. Rosales (eds) *Interculturalidad y Bilingüismo en la Formación de Recursos*

Humanos: Educación, Medicina, Derecho y Etnodesarrollo. Lima: CILA, Universidad Nacional Mayor de San Marcos.

Rosales, M. (2009) La formación de docentes EIB en La Cantuta. In *Encuentro Nacional de Pedagogía Intercultural desde Los Pueblos*. Lima: Universidad Nacional Mayor de San Marcos, CILA, ANAMEBI.

Schensul, J.J. and Schensul, S.L. (1992) Collaborative research: Methods of inquiry for social change. In M.D. Le Compte, W.L. Millroy and J. Preissle (eds) *The Handbook of Qualitative Research in Education*. London: Academic Press.

Suxo, M. (2005) La zona de desarrollo próximo en el aprendizaje del niño aimara. In *Revista de Educación Intercultural Bilingüe Qinasay* (Vol. 3). Cochabamba: Universidad Mayor De San Simón.

Suxo, M. (in press) La interculturalidad en la universidad peruana. Preliminary Research Report. Lima.

Tuhiwai Smith, L. (2002) *Decolonizing Methodologies: Research and Indigenous Peoples*. London: Zed Books.

Chapter 4
Education and Social Justice in Neoliberal Times: Historical and Pedagogical Perspectives from Two Postcolonial Contexts

MATTHEW CLARKE and BRIAN MORGAN

> It was intended that when Newspeak had been adopted once and for all and the Oldspeak forgotten, a heretical thought ... should be literally unthinkable, at least so far as thought is dependent on words.
> George Orwell, *1984*

Introduction

The dystopian future imagined by Orwell in his infamous masterpiece, *1984*, it should be remembered, was borne of the hypocrisies that Orwell [Eric Blair] witnessed as a volunteer during the Spanish Civil War and later described in *Homage to Catalonia*. Spain, as the international frontline against fascism, offered clear purpose for the young men who answered the Republican call to arms. Yet, the war unfolded in ways that shattered many ideals, with ideologically fragmented and disorganized militias on the left as prone to attacking or sacrificing each other as they were to engaging with their fascist enemies on the right. It was a historical setting in which language was mobilized to do many things: to paper over uncompromising differences, to demonize those who once were compatriots and to proclaim unassailable 'truths' when few were readily apparent – in sum, the essence of what we often call propaganda when deployed by opponents.

Orwell's provocative notion of Newspeak, in which 'thought is dependent on words', foregrounds what we see as an area of particular specialization for language teacher educators who wish to integrate social justice concerns within their curricula. In common cause, such curricula would seek to raise teachers' awareness of racism, sexism, homophobia, economic and environmental exploitation and the ways in which they influence pedagogy and constrain students' life chances beyond the classroom. At the same time, such curricula from a second language education (SLE) perspective would apply analytic rigor to the 'dependency on language' that Orwell articulates. In this regard, it is important to consider that propaganda, discourses and ideologies are, to a large degree, linguistic constructions, whereby grammatical and lexical choices influence self and collective identity and shape how citizens perceive and act upon notions of social justice and the common good (e.g. Morgan & Vandrick, 2009). Second and foreign language settings, where language is both the *medium* and *object* of analysis, draw on the fact that in comparison to monolinguals, bi- and multilingual speakers are more aware of the ways in which 'realities' and 'possibilities' change through their representation in different languages and uses of languages. In addition, these settings are also unique for the diverse student experiences available to inspire a social justice unit or syllabus. As Morgan and Vandrick (2009) note, English as a Second Language (ESL)/English for Academic Purposes (EAP) 'contact zones' are often sites in which, for example, the personal accounts of historical enemies or the experiences of racialized and marginalized 'others' are first encountered. Indeed, the conversations and practices generated in such settings offer an 'outsider's' perspective on social justice issues no longer available to more long-standing citizens whose internalization of dominant discourses (systemic meritocracy and color-blindness, for example) preclude a critical distance with which to assess the interests and actions of powerful decision makers.

A social justice agenda, when informed by SLE, can also draw upon an elaborate research literature in second language acquisition (SLA), attentive to how thoughts and words (cf. Orwell) are correlated both causally and contextually – how the learning and internalization of values and beliefs related to social justice are shaped by cognitive and semiotic processes, both conscious and unconscious, intentional and incidental, immediate and recursive. More than ever, recent SLA research and the (post)methodologies (cf. Kumaravadivelu, 2003) that arise from them emphasize a 'social turn' in the field (cf. Block, 2003), one in which local contingencies, sociocultural practices and relations of power are integral to language learning.

In this relatively new conceptualization, language teachers, and the practices and relationships they organize, have a more central role in how SLA occurs (e.g. Block, 2003; van Lier, 2004) than was the case prior to the 'social' and 'linguistic' turns. In short, the current research and pedagogical agenda in SLE convincingly frames language as a social practice and advances the legitimacy and agency of L2 teachers in promoting a language and text-based approach to social justice pedagogies.

Still, for language teacher educators who wish to promote this critical potential in their preservice settings, ideological and institutional barriers make this utilization in Language Teacher Education (LTE) difficult to achieve. Across both our sites of professional work – Australia and Canada – a common barrier we experience is a reform agenda intent on achieving greater efficiencies, accountability and competitiveness in program delivery. This pressure 'to subject teacher education to market forces', as Zeichner notes in his introductory chapter, is often referred to as neoliberalism, to which we now turn our discussion.

The Neoliberal Agenda

The term neoliberalism itself can be confusing in North American contexts, where contemporary liberalism refers to a more activist role for government in the management of social and fiscal policy. The historical antecedents are radically different, however, dating back to the *laissez-faire*, noninterventionist ideals of 18th century British philosophers such as Adam Smith and David Ricardo – a legacy reflected in current *neo*liberal actions that seek to downsize the function and role of nation-state governments through reduced taxation, deregulation and privatization of economic activity (Steger, 2003).

In the wake of globalization and the expansion of global media networks, neoliberal values, including 'choice', 'freedom', 'standards', 'accountability' and a belief in the all-powerful forces of 'free trade' and 'the market', have become hegemonic in societies across the world. In education this has led to profound consequences for conceptions of teaching, learning, research, knowledge and, of particular concern for this chapter, language. Indeed, neoliberalism thinking is underpinned by what we might call an 'empiricist/idealist' notion of language, in which language bears a direct and complete relation to 'experience', which is directly and unproblematically communicated and understood by a transcendent, prelinguistic individual (Olssen *et al.*, 2004: 63). As Olssen *et al.* point out, what this results in is a politically debilitating failure to recognize the sociality of language and the pervasive and inherent presence of issues of power and politics in language practices. The need for such recognition is central to our argument in this chapter. By understanding and/or teaching language as 'objective tool' and as 'innocent medium', as Morgan (1987) observes, 'the agency of the speaker is drastically curtailed, reduced to selecting the correct expression from the pregiven alternatives offered' (p. 450). Such assumptions are inimical to a social justice agenda in LTE, one in which issues of power and agency are addressed throughout the curriculum.

Although the idealist/empiricist notion of language above has antecedents long before capitalism, it is instructive to recognize the extent to which they align with the economistic dimensions of a neoliberal agenda, one in which language increasingly becomes both tool and commodity in the service of a globalized knowledge economy. And as with the division of labor in prior modes of industrial production, language becomes 'alienated' (cf. Marx) from its speakers/owners, objectified and subjected to the techniques of scientific management (cf. Taylorism; Braverman, 1974) whereby discrete elements of language work (e.g. pragmatics, phonology, lexicogrammar) are analyzed and monitored in search of greater efficiencies. A prominent example would be the current growth in so-called 'accent neutrality' courses and the normalization of North American discourse norms for Indian call center employees (Cowie, 2007; Ramanathan & Morgan, 2009).

Indeed, it is instructive to contrast neoliberalism with a social justice approach to education across a number of areas, including language, the subject, knowledge and the purposes of education. As noted above, neoliberalism is underpinned by an objectivist view, which sees language as a transparent and neutral medium for reflecting a pregiven reality and communicating thought. By contrast, social justice approaches see language as an inherently social phenomenon that is constructive of reality, social relations and identities as well as intimately connected to issues of power and ideology. In this view, language and social phenomena exist in a dialogic relationship, as language comes to carry traces, accents and meanings through the social uses of its speakers and speaking communities. Language is 'situated' and users seen as active meaning-makers, (re)creating the media, texts and signs that they utilize. Likewise, whereas neoliberalism assumes a view of the subject as universal and hence preexisting and transcending language and society, for social justice approaches individuals are discursively and socially formed, shaped differently in different situations, times and places. As a logical correlative of its view of language and of the individual, neoliberalism sees knowledge as objective and atomized, something that can be transmitted unchanged and parcel-like from one discrete individual mind to another, whereas social justice approaches recognize the partial, situated and dialogic nature of knowledge, emphasizing how it is always co-implicated in relations of power as different parties contest the right to define reality and society. Finally, in line with its objectivist epistemology and its ironically deeply political, 'apolitical' assumptions, neoliberalism takes a detached, instrumentalist and utilitarian view of the purposes of education that could be paraphrased as a matter of increasing the greatest number of test scores for the greatest number of students; by contrast, social justice approaches are imbued with concern for equity and fairness across a range of domains and the potential for education to contribute toward that goal.

Sadly, as Zeichner notes in his chapter in this volume, the neoliberal view has become hegemonic in education systems across the world. Luke *et al.* (2007) aptly describe the neoliberal hegemony as 'a planetary "newspeak" that lines the pages of newspapers, blogs, and screens with the language of the "market", and with its images and discourses of competitive and possessive individualism' (Luke *et al.*, 2007: 4) – which has led to the ascendancy of business and market ideologies in education generally (Luke, 2006; Marginson, 2006; Sleeter, 2007), as well as in teacher education and professional development (Cochran-Smith, 2005; Day, 2007), and, of particular concern for this chapter, language education (Chun, 2009; Corson, 2001; Harvey, 2006; Holborow, 2007; Jordao, 2009; Phillipson, 2008). This ascendancy is often justified by those slippery signifiers, 'reform' and 'standards' (Apple, 2001b) and underpinned by the deployment of a particular set of discursive strategies, for example 'the evidentiary warrant' that values 'empirical' over 'ideological' positions, 'the accountability warrant' that values 'outputs' over 'inputs' and 'the political warrant' that purportedly values 'public' over 'private'[1] benefits in education (Cochran-Smith & Fries, 2001). These signifiers – just some examples of neoliberal newspeak – and strategies deny their own ideological contingency and present themselves as universal and unchallengeable truth.

Criticisms leveled against the hegemonic influence of neoliberal ideologies in relation to the work of teachers in recent years include charges that they reduce diversity, undermine professionalism and 'attempt to rebrand teachers as "servants of the state" merely carrying out public policy' rather than 'public intellectuals' (Grimmett *et al.*, 2009: 5); and that they have led to 'increased bureaucratic scrutiny directed towards the work of schools and teachers ... contributing to significant work intensification' (Bloomfield, 2009: 34). As Hill bluntly and forcefully states, 'teachers are being controlled!' (2007: 212). Such bureaucratic scrutiny is facilitated by the articulation of performance indicators and standards that seek 'to specify, often in distressing detail, what students, teachers and future teachers should be able to know, say and do' (Apple, 2001a: 188). In the specific context of teacher education, commentators have criticized the neoliberal 'accreditation squeeze', which is 'trivializing teacher education' in global contexts as diverse as the United States and the United Arab of Emirates (Johnson et al., 2005). Meanwhile, in relation to pupils, critics have pointed out how neoliberal educational policies and practices have brought in their wake 'emphases on technical and managerial solutions to moral and political problems' along with 'a subtle but crucial shift in emphasis ... from student needs to student performance and from what the school does for the student to what the student does for the school' (Apple, 2001a: 182, 185). These latter shifts can be seen, for example, in concerns about performance in local and national league tables that evaluate and record the school's value in the educational marketplace and in the growing emphasis on marketing and publicity that seek to distinguish schools in relation to their competitors.

Of course, neoliberal reforms in education are not as entirely malevolent and mendacious as the above picture implies; they were motivated by desire for, and have not been without benefits in relation to, greater openness, transparency, accountability and communication in relation to educational quality and standards; and it is in such terms that contemporary neoliberal politicians defend neoliberal reforms. Thus, for example, in a speech entitled 'Accountable government, accountable communities: The role of transparency in education reform', then Workplace Relations and Education Minister, Julia Gillard, describing the Australian government's *My School* website, emphasized how 'this website will allow users to compare one school's results with schools around the nation that serve similar student populations. It will show how a school's test scores compare to those statistically similar schools and to the national mean' (Gillard, 2009). The assumption here is that increased visibility, transparency and accountability will lead to rising standards and promote equality of access in education. Yet as a growing body of literature indicates – and the above citations are but a small sample of this literature – the drive for accountability and transparency has not produced the heralded improvements in standards (Mills, 2008). Instead, it has led to a number of unforeseen results. These include the phenomenon of middle class flight from state education in the United Kingdom, Australia and elsewhere under the banner of 'choice' (Ball, 2003), as well as a narrowing of education, in terms of curriculum, and in relation to conceptions of what it means to be an educated person (Sleeter, 2007) – as well as what it means to be a teacher – leading one commentator to talk of the 'rampant normalization associated with high stakes accountability' (Gunzenhauser, 2008: 2237).

For a number of reasons, language education has been particularly vulnerable to the underlying ontological, epistemological and ethical assumptions of neoliberalism, with its emphasis on quantification and measurability. These reasons include the tendency of linguists and language educators to objectify languages and demarcate them as discrete, enumerative entities, each with a homogeneous and hermetic population ascribed to it; their atomistic and asocial view of languages as comprising collections of rules and structures; and the emphasis on the sovereignty of the rational individual language user (Block, 2003; Reagan, 2004). As Reagan notes, 'linguists and language specialists, as well as the lay public, have generally viewed language from a perspective that is, at its heart, fundamentally positivist in orientation. We have tended to assume that language as an abstract entity ... exists as just such a knowable entity' (2004: 42). It can be argued that such objectifying, reificatory approaches lend themselves to the commodification of language and resonate with the technicist, rationalistic and instrumental views of education dominant in neoliberal regimes. Such views serve to depoliticize language education, detaching it from issues of privilege, power, access and discrimination and instead portraying it as something, in Pennycook's (1994: 38) words, that is 'natural, neutral, and beneficial'. In the following sections we explore the challenges of confronting this mindset in teacher education in two physically distant but 'discursively' related contexts.

Perspectives from Two Postcolonial Contexts: Australia

As we noted above, social justice approaches to teacher education are concerned with issues of discrimination across a range of areas, including race, ethnicity, class, gender and sexuality, and with the social patterns and political decisions that connect discrimination and disadvantage across these domains. All these issues remain ongoing challenges for Australian society. However, events such as the racially motivated Cronulla riots of 2005, the recent spate of attacks, some fatal, on Indian students in Australian cities, and – notwithstanding the laudable apology by the Australian federal government in 2007 for the forced removal of Aboriginal and Torres Strait Islander children from their families that was an official government policy from 1909 to 1969 – the ongoing socioeconomic abjection of Australia's Aboriginal communities, all remind us that Leonardo's comment that 'racism is central to understanding the American landscape and history' (2009: 240) is also true for Australia. Indeed, despite the prominence accorded to the United States and United Kingdom as imperial/neo-imperial powers in discussions of racial and ethnic discrimination, a case can be made that Australia pointed the way toward education and literacy as technologies for inscribing the binary lines that demarcated whiteness from its 'others' when 'at the beginning of the twentieth century, Australians drew a colour line around their continent and declared whiteness to be at the very heart of their national identity' (Lake & Reynolds, 2008: 138).

During the inaugural parliament of 1901, Australia's first federal legislators passed the Immigration Restriction Act as a means to prevent 'nonwhites' from settling in Australia. In order to circumvent imperial restrictions on racially discriminatory immigration legislation, a literacy test was mandated for all persons wishing to enter Australia. But as Lake and Reynolds note, 'paradoxically, the implementation of a literacy test framed to avoid all reference to race helped consolidate the new binary divide between the "white" and "non-white" races, a purpose made explicit in Australian parliamentary debate and the legislation passed to enact White Australia' (2008: 146).

This episode can be read as emblematic of the implication of language and literacy education in the politics of discrimination and of the masquerading of inequality behind the rhetoric of universalism, themes which are as germane today as they were 100 years ago. Thus, for example, when former Australian Prime Minister John Howard took office in 1995 he declared that his government would be one that represented 'all Australians', asserting a mantle of universal representativeness that many politicians lay claim to in order to establish their legitimacy. Yet despite the universalist rhetoric, his government (1996–2007) accelerated the neoliberal trends initiated by his predecessors, introducing policies which advantaged the wealthy and middle classes while scapegoating and stoking hostility toward less advantaged groups, such as Aboriginal Australians, the unemployed, immigrants and asylum seekers, who were positioned in the popular media as blameworthy for the challenges they faced and responsible for their own fate in society. This reading of social disadvantage is consonant with the neoliberal view that citizens are rational, autonomous, individual actors whose interests are best served when they are freed from the heavy hand of coercive government intervention, which is how policies targeting inequality are characterized in the neoliberal worldview. In the wake of such interventionist government programs, free markets are advocated as the mechanism that best enables individuals to exercise autonomy and in turn produces the most effective and efficient economic outcomes for society.

We can see the emergence and increasing hegemony of this neoliberal, human-capital informed view when we look at the specific areas of multicultural and language policies [2] in Australia, where an emphasis on managing both diversity and national social cohesion has been replaced by an instrumental focus on economic advantage. Thus we can contrast 1989's government discussion paper, 'National Agenda for Multicultural Australia', which examined how Australia can accommodate diversity and difference, with 2006's 'Discussion Paper on Citizenship Testing', which was premised on what immigrants can do for Australia. The latter paper proposed (and its recommendations were subsequently adopted) testing in English language proficiency and in commitment to 'Australian values'. We can also see this neoliberal shift in the recent promotion of 'economically useful' languages (e.g. Japanese, Chinese, Indonesian, Korean, German and French) at the expense of implicitly less useful 'community languages' (e.g. Arabic, Greek and Vietnamese) (Liddicoat, 2009).

Ironically, given this emphasis on English language proficiency, the links usually asserted between English and economic well-being and the Federal government's responsibility for immigration, funding for the provision of ESL in schools has been steadily eroded in recent years. Most notably, in 1998 under the banner of the *Literacy for All* policy, specific Federal funding to meet the ESL needs of all but immediate new arrivals was 'broadbanded', or 'displaced', into enhanced literacy funding, much of which was linked to national literacy benchmarking tests (Cross, 2009; Michell, 1999). Similar tactics were used by newly elected Prime Minister Kevin Rudd when he removed Federal funding for ESL provision for new arrivals in 2008 under the broader banner of his 'Education Revolution', which, beyond its high-profile provision of laptops to grade 9 students, seems little more than a continuation of the previous government's backlash against 'progressive' education in the name of privatization, competition and an emphasis on 'the basics' (Hattam *et al.*, 2009). Even prior to this coup de grace, ESL planning, advocacy and provision at both state and federal levels had been hamstrung by the cessation of the collection of national statistics on newly arrived students since 2000, creating an effective 'data blackout' (Michell, 2009: 3).

As a result of these successive policy 'evacuations', any ESL provision that remains available for children in Australian schools is offered by state governments, over and above any formal legal obligation; hence, ESL students are left 'without any specialist or ongoing support to address their specific needs as non-native-speaking students in the mainstream curriculum' in a policy context that emphasizes 'homogeneity and the maintenance of the existing social order, rather than the recognition or acceptance of linguistic and cultural diversity' (Cross, 2009: 519).

Within this overall pattern of social injustice, particular concern has been raised and/or reiterated in recent years about a number of social justice issues in Australian society. These include rising levels of Islamophobia (Dunn *et al.*, 2007; Forrest & Dunn, 2006) and the damaging effect this is having on the educational opportunities of students of Arab-Islamic backgrounds, who find themselves increasingly disengaged and disenfranchised in relation to the social and economic benefits of schooling (Kamp & Mansouri, 2009; Mansouri & Wood, 2008; Welch, 2007). They also include moral panics about the prospect of mainstream Australian society being overwhelmed by 'floods' of refugees and asylum seekers, many of whom in recent years are Muslims from countries ravaged by Western neo-imperialist adventures (Matthews, 2008). Meanwhile, in spite of various forms of welfare support intended to overcome two centuries of 'disease, dispossession and violence' (Lake & Reynolds, 2008: 15), the educational and economic underachievement of indigenous Australians reflects the continuing prevalence of 'indisputable economic injustice and widespread social exclusion, cultural denial and denigration' whereby 'long-standing injustices are rescripted and reinscribed through their links with contemporary scapes of abjection' (Kenway & Hickey-Moody, 2009: 98, 104).

Neoliberal regimes mask and perpetuate these injustices through their denial of difference and insistence on formal equality (i.e. same treatment) rather than equity (i.e. treatment in accordance with needs and characteristics) (Hall, 2009) as well as through their exclusion of 'politics' as a strategy for asserting the hegemony of the status quo. These are tendencies that teacher education for social justice needs to challenge and resist.

Matthew's course in Australia

In the teacher education program Matthew teaches in Australia, these issues are addressed in a course entitled Culture, Identity and Education. The students taking this course come from a variety of teaching disciplines, with some preparing to teach history, others preparing to teach physics, and only a minority training as ESL teachers; but a foundational premise of the course is that 'language matters', whatever discipline they might teach (Ninnes, 2009). The students are introduced to a poststructuralist conceptual lens to assist them in recognizing the multiple ways of perceiving reality that reflect differences in social and cultural experiences, to help them to see that all truth claims are inevitably situated and partial and to encourage them to 'read' discursive statements in the social, material and historical contexts from which they emerge. These aims echo the title of a recent book on teaching for social justice as being a matter of 'interrogating common sense' (Soliman, 2009). Throughout the course, students use their emerging 'meta-discursive' awareness to critique representations of social, cultural and national identities in media and educational texts by identifying the exclusions and assumptions these texts rely upon to stake their claims, and by naming the specific interests lying behind claims to disinterested universality. Thus, to provide one small example, we noted how a newspaper article that was published during the course positioned Aboriginal youth as threatening outsiders beyond the pale of civilization through such constructions as 'the public needs to feel safe that these people are behind bars and kept away from society' (Owen & Nason, 2009: 2) and how the repeated discursive performance of such essentializing dichotomies in media and educational texts works to establish a perpetual, pervasive and pernicious 'othering' (Ninnes, 2009), restricting Aboriginal identities to 'abject zones' (Kenway & Hickey-Moody, 2009: 97). Such activities, focused on detailed work at the level of language and discourse, attempt to take up the challenge laid down to teacher education programs by Zeichner in this volume to work toward lessening social, political and economic inequalities in education and in wider society.

The course underlines the importance of recognizing and affirming diversity and difference in relation to views and backgrounds and of incorporating and building on students' social and cultural experiences when designing curriculum, while also extending students beyond the familiar and providing them with a mastery of socially powerful forms of knowledge. Students are encouraged to see themselves as public intellectuals rather than as transmitters of state curriculum, and this is reflected in the main assignment of the course, which is to develop a 'blueprint for action' to address a social justice issue. This can take the form of a workshop for teachers or a curriculum unit on issues related to culture and identity, to name just a few possibilities. As one example of student responses to this challenge, which relates to the above discussion of the removal of federally funded ESL provision in Australian schools, a group of students created a project, which involved a community action campaign targeting students, parents, teachers, principals, community leaders and political representatives, to raise awareness about the need for increased resources to meet the needs of ESL students. The campaign included information packs about the lack of ESL provision in schools, and the negative effects this is having in terms of social justice, along with a petition urging the Federal Minister for Education to dramatically increase funding for ESL students. The students framed their project as the result of dismay at the inadequacy of ESL provision they encountered during teaching practice placements.

So far the course has been taught in its current format just once and feedback from students was largely positive with constructive suggestions for improvement, most notably for a greater emphasis on positive examples of social justice work on the part of teachers in schools. However, noting Zeichner's comments in the chapter in this volume, which echo comments made by student teachers in the course, scope for further development is clear. For example, the assignment would be far more powerful if students are expected to carry out, rather than just plan, their blueprint, so as to marry theory and practice more effectively. Beyond this, as Zeichner emphasizes in his chapter, it is worth noting the limitation of innovations at the classroom level and the importance of embedding social justice concerns at the program level, as well as emulating neoliberalism's success in influencing the policy agenda at a system level. Meeting this challenge requires that teachers at both university and school resist neoliberalism's casting of them as technicians of externally mandated curriculum and reclaim their status as public intellectuals.

Perspectives from Two Postcolonial Contexts: Canada

In ways parallel to the Australian experience, Canada was established through the systematic dispossession of aboriginal lands to facilitate white settlement, followed by paternalistic efforts to 'civilize' aboriginal peoples and eradicate their languages and cultures through an enforced and abusive residential school system (Warnock, 2004: Ch. 7) – a policy for which the Federal government officially apologized and offered compensation. Also similarly, until the 1960s, Canada maintained race-based and geographical restrictions/quotas on immigration, these reflecting commonsense views regarding the kinds of newcomers deemed most desirable and capable of assimilating to the Anglo-centric norms of the nation (Palmer, 1976). Since the 1960s, discrimination based on identity/geography has been replaced by more subtle forms of exclusion whereby Canadian immigration policy now favors newcomers with higher education, professional skills or investment means, a reflection of an aging population and sector-specific labor shortages at home, but also a forecasting of future needs in a globalized economy.

Still, there are also notable Canadian particularities that have informed Canada's social justice agenda and the kinds of issues and content to consider for LTE and SLE settings. The emergence of official multiculturalism in Canada, for example, was a reaction to Anglo-French hegemony in the national narrative, a backlash on the part of second- and third-generation immigrants from Central and Eastern Europe against the 1963 Royal Commission on Bilingualism and Biculturalism, whose 'terms of reference seemed to place non-British and non-French groups into a category of second-class citizens' (Palmer, 1976: 516). The compromise that was later achieved – a multicultural policy within the framework of official English–French bilingualism – has been viewed by many critics as ineffective if not patronizing in its superficiality (e.g. 'culture Disneyfied'; Bissoondath, 1994), leaving long-standing structures of power and inequality in the society unchallenged. Yet, this might be too narrow an assessment in that official multiculturalism has also served to legitimate and support a 'politics of recognition' (cf. Taylor, in Fraser, 1997), whereby well-organized ethnolinguistic groups have utilized state resources not only for the preservation of heritage languages and cultures but also for the astute promotion of the political and economic interests of their communities. The apparent commercial self-interest behind such strategies, however, should be viewed within a larger, more supportive context: the neoliberal rebranding of Canada's ethnolinguistic diversity as an entrepreneurial resource, an official shift most prominently marked by the 'Multiculturalism Means Business' conference held in Toronto in 1986 and presided over by the Prime Minister of the day, Brian Mulroney. As Williams' (1998) summary of the conference indicates:

> From the Canadian government's perspective the message is clear; multiculturalism is not only about preserving cultures and improving race relations, it is also about extending trade relations, about employment, about science and technology, global linkage. (p. 22)

This federal shift in priorities meant that the social justice needs of a multicultural/multiracial society would be balanced against and sometimes subordinated to the economic opportunities ethnolinguistic diversity provided. The subsequent rebranding and commodification of multiculturalism has had a profound impact on both the content and provision of adult ESL in Canada. Since the 1990s, the Federal government has attempted to increase system-wide efficiency and accountability in the provision of adult ESL, first through the creation of the Canadian Language Benchmarks (CLBs), a 12-benchmark descriptive scale of task-based language proficiencies for standardized assessment and ESL course placement, followed by the Language Instruction to Newcomers to Canada (LINC) program, which is based on the CLB and serves as the basic structure of adult ESL programming and curricula in most Canadian provinces (Fleming, 2007). Whereas earlier LINC curricula integrated a broad thematic range of settlement language needs, including citizenship and equity topics (see, e.g. Pinet, 2006; Thomson & Derwing, 2004), recent documents (e.g. LINC 5-7 Curriculum Guidelines, 2007, Citizenship and Immigration Canada) now prominently favor job-related language skills, a trend that reflects the federal government's efforts in correlating recent immigrant employment policies with the CLB model. As Gibb's (2008) analysis of the resulting 2005 *Comparative Framework* indicates, the newly integrated policy text 'reveals human capital theory and the knowledge economy as the dominant discourses ... marginalizing the social and structural complexities of second language learning in adulthood' (p. 318).

What is remarkable and consistent in these documents is the discursive construction of language as the sole obstacle/barrier to participation in the economy and social mobility – hence, an obstacle for which newcomers/learners and language providers are held primarily responsible. Missing from this discursive frame are the persistent systemic barriers that new immigrants and visible minorities face in having their foreign credentials recognized by Canadian professional associations and their prior experiences valued in Canadian workplaces (Keung, 2007; Lewington, 2009).

For Canadian adult ESL instructors, this enhanced responsibility for newcomer 'success' comes during a gradual decline in job security and working conditions, a predictable outcome of the Federal government's 'deregulation agenda' (cf. Zeichner) achieved through increased privatization of LINC programming (see, e.g. Burnaby, 2002; Fleming, 2007; Haque & Cray, 2007). Meanwhile, and consistent with the 'professionalization agenda' described by Zeichner, the certification requirements for prospective adult ESL teachers are relatively expensive and highly regulated by a centralized, provincial licensing body, the TESL Ontario organization (e.g. see TESL Ontario's certification criteria on http://www.teslontario.org/certification/). This chapter now turns to a discussion of Brian's preservice LTE course within the TESL Ontario certification program and his particular efforts at integrating a social justice component with the constraints and possibilities described above.

Brian's course in Canada

'Socio-Political Issues in Second Language Teaching' (LING 3600.3) is a three-credit, 12-week course, required as part of the 30-credit York University TESOL Certificate Programme (e.g. http://www.yorku.ca/laps/dlll/tesol/). Similar to Matthew's course in Australia, Brian's course readings attempt to instill a poststructural perspective on language, emphasizing its role in identity negotiation and power relations within and beyond the classroom. Teacher agency in the construction of course knowledge is also foregrounded through the course readings and discussions. As a preservice LTE course, readings also take up social justice issues specific to students' emerging professional lives: the geopolitics of English, language ideologies regarding native speakerness and standard languages, and the professional marginalization of the so-called non-native-speaking teachers of English. Issues specific to the content and provision of Canadian ESL, as described in the section above, are also featured prominently in the course syllabus.

A detailed outline of this course, including weekly readings and assignments, can be found in a recent publication (Morgan, 2009). Some of the course themes that the readings cover include the geopolitics of English as an international language; adult ESL policies and practices in Canada; the politics of classrooms, teachers and students; ideologies of language and identity in ELT classrooms; the politics and ethics of ELT testing and assessment; the possibilities and limitations for critical teaching and curriculum/syllabus design; and, in the last week, the importance of developing leadership and advocacy skills. For the remainder of this section, the focus will be on the final assignment for the course, a group project called the Issues Analysis Project (IAP). The following descriptions from the assignment handout illustrate the scope and social justice aspirations for the IAP:

- The premise of this assignment is that the effective teacher is aware of the sociopolitical context within which she or he works. It also assumes that the instructor has a professional responsibility to attempt to deal with the issues that impact negatively on the teaching–learning process and the situation of second language learners and teachers.
- The objective of this assignment is to select an issue and structure a response that will at least in some way work toward resolving the issue. In other words, you will produce a blueprint for action that is responsive to the issue identified and could, at least in theory, be carried out as proposed. Your response might be in the form of a

new policy, advocacy initiative, curriculum innovation, specialized materials or an in-service/preservice workshop for teachers and/or program administrators.

Beginning around the sixth or seventh week of the course, class time is set aside for groups to work on their projects, to share their problems and progress and to examine effective 'blueprints for action' – often exemplary IAPs from previous years – given the audience and textual medium/format chosen. In class, students are encouraged to relate their projects to the social and professional gaps/problems they are observing as part of their practicum program, concurrent with the sociopolitics course. As well, students whose IAPs take the form of lesson plans or units are encouraged to conceptualize the integration of social justice issues within a task-based, thematic second language syllabus, as modeled on the LINC curricula documents and the CLBs.

Over the years, there have been many examples of IAPs that illustrate a social justice awareness applied to the specificities of adult ESL and EAP programming. From the last year Brian taught the course (Winter 2009), two warrant specific mentions for their content and the way they address the neoliberal agenda that frames this chapter. The first was conceptualized and organized by three students. Its title is LVR (Listings of Valuable Resources for Immigrants' Access to Rights in Canada: An Introductory Resource Guide on How to Address Immigrants' Social Concerns in the Canadian Classroom). As the title indicates, this IAP serves as a reference guide for ESL teachers, often asked but rarely prepared or trained to offer advice or adequate referral to the many settlement needs of newcomers. The LVR features information on the Canadian Charter of Rights and Freedom, Ontario Human Rights Act, Employment Standards Act, Landlord and Tenant Rights, and a comprehensive list of websites, resources and social agencies for newcomers in need of assistance. It is an effective resource, both for its content and the way it reminds ESL teachers of the extralinguistic, social needs of students, which are currently subordinated to the prioritization of job-specific language skills in government policy statements and LINC curricula (Gibb, 2008; Morgan & Fleming, 2009).

The second IPA of note takes up problems related to the professionalization agenda identified by Zeichner. The blueprint for action comes in the form of an advocacy letter to the university arguing for the creation of a Master's in TESOL to replace the existing undergraduate TESOL certificate. As this group of four students persuasively argued, the rapid expansion of TESOL certification programs throughout the world has increased the supply of qualified teachers, giving those with Master's degrees additional advantages in securing better positions overseas. This group then researched the course requirements of several MA-TESOL programs in the United States, finding these programs to be equivalent in duration and theoretical depth with the undergraduate certificate offered at York University. There are points that can be made for and against this advocacy proposal. To what extent should universities participate in the 'devaluation' of their degrees and diplomas in order to be competitive with other certifying institutions? At the same time, to what extent can universities and program administrators ignore the financial and professional pressures that students experience as a consequence of programs whose structures are anchored within institutional exigencies and slow to respond to external realities? At the least, this provocative IAP draws critical attention to the kinds of neoliberal pressures that are currently shaping the SLE profession and that a social justice agenda in LTE must address.

Conclusion: Teacher Education and Social Justice Concerns

The instrumentalism that is part and parcel of the global entrenchment of neoliberalism – for as Braidotti (2006: 1) comments, 'times are definitely no longer a-changing' – involving the prevalence of discourses promoting a view of teaching as a matter of meeting centrally prescribed performance criteria, and the narrowing effect that this, along with the overwhelming torrent of accountability-driven educational reform, is having on teacher professionalism, all combine to severely limit the space and scope for exploring social justice concerns (Lynn & Smith-Maddox, 2007). In this context, it seems clear that teacher educators need to explore alternative models that offer scope for reclaiming and revitalizing our professional formation and development as individuals and as communities committed to inclusion and democracy, rather than just as anonymous copies of a centralized blueprint for what it means to be a teacher. As we noted in our initial discussion of Orwellian newspeak, a critical meta-awareness of language and discourse is central to this challenge. Thus teachers need to recognize, question and challenge the underlying assumptions and 'blind-spots', values and beliefs, inclusions and exclusions, inhering in contemporary neoliberal 'newspeak'. However, this involves not only recognizing and critiquing the operations of this particular discourse but also developing critical awareness of the strategic moves, operations and wider 'games' of discourse per se. As

Gee puts it, 'teachers must not only be masters of the Discourse or Discourses to which they are apprenticing their learners, they must be masters, as well, of what we might call the "political geography of Discourses" ' (Gee, 2004: 30). This is indeed a significant challenge and one to which language education brings particular strengths, for example its detailed vocabulary and conceptual frameworks for describing and analyzing language practices, as well as potential weaknesses, for example the tendency in the field we noted earlier to see language as an objective, commodifiable entity or 'thing'.

But language and discourse are only part of the battle. As Zeichner stresses in his chapter, meeting the challenges of social justice in teacher education requires work at all levels within and across our institutions as well as beyond, into the political and public arenas. Without such efforts, we run the risk of 'simply adopt[ing] the label of social justice without challenging or changing existing practices' (McDonald & Zeichner, 2009: 606). Unfortunately we have a long way to go in this regard and attempts to address issues of discrimination and difference in teacher education programs have often been critiqued as 'fragmented and superficial' (Mills & Ballantyne, 2009: 1). Indeed, as noted above, the intensification associated with neoliberal accountability regimes increasingly squeezes such concerns out of the curriculum, as does neoliberalism's preference for formal equality over substantive equity and its strategic exclusion of the 'political'. Despite these pressures, a number of teacher education researchers have sought to address the distinct but related concerns of teacher attrition and increasing intercultural diversity in schools. Some of this work has focused on working with preservice or novice teachers' dispositions (Mills, 2006; Talbert-Johnson, 2006; Villegas, 2007) in recognition of the central significance of awareness of self and identity in building openness to difference (Mills & Ballantyne, 2009; Santoro & Allard, 2005). Other work, recognizing the pivotal place of 'voice' in critical race theory and the importance of working at multiple levels in order to effect change, has sought to raise teachers' awareness of the often hidden patterns of discrimination that lie behind 'business as usual' in education and to engage them in frank and open dialogue with a range of stakeholders including students, peers, principals, parents and community leaders (Kamp & Mansouri, 2009). Our own two stories are but a small part of this wider effort; nonetheless, our hope is that they might provide some source of succor, hope and encouragement to others in joining us in this critical endeavor.

Notes

1. Although neoliberalism is usually associated with the promotion of the 'private' sphere, what Cochran-Smith and Fries describe here is a contemporary example of 'newspeak', where advocates for the deregulation of teaching claim that they are championing openness and democracy in the name of the 'public' good while depicting their ideological 'adversaries' (i.e. teachers' unions, educational researchers and academics) as advancing narrow, 'private' self-interests.
2. Liddicoat (2009) notes that the latter grew out of the former in Australia, though it has since developed its own discourses.

References

Apple, M. (2001a) Markets, standards, teaching, and teacher education. *Journal of Teacher Education* 52 (2), 182–196.
Apple, M. (2001b) Will standards save public education? *Educational Policy* 15 (5), 724–729.
Ball, S. (2003) *Class Strategies and the Education Market: The Middle Classes and Social Advantage*. London: Routledge.
Bissoondath, N. (1994) *Selling Illusions: The Cult of Multiculturalism in Canada*. Toronto: Penguin.
Block, D. (2003) *The Social Turn in Second Language Acquisition*. Edinburgh: Edinburgh University Press.
Bloomfield, D. (2009) Working within and against neoliberal accreditation agendas: Opportunities for professional experience. *Asia-Pacific Journal of Teacher Education* 37 (1), 27–44.
Braidotti, R. (2006) *Transpositions: On Nomadic Ethics*. Cambridge: Polity Press.
Braverman, H. (1974) *Labour and Monopoly Capital: The Degradation of Work in the Twentieth Century*. New York: Monthly Review Press.
Burnaby, B. (2002) Reflections on language policies in Canada: Three examples. In J.W. Tollefson (ed.) *Language Policies in Education* (pp. 65–86). Mahwah, NJ: Erlbaum.
Chun, C.W. (2009) Contesting neoliberal discourses in EAP: Critical praxis in an IEP classroom. *Journal of English for Academic Purposes* 8 (2), 111–120.
Cochran-Smith, M. (2005) The new teacher education: For better or for worse? *Educational Researcher* 34 (7), 3–17.
Cochran-Smith, M. and Fries, M. (2001) Sticks, stones, and ideology: The discourse of reform in teacher education. *Educational Researcher* 30 (8), 3–15.
Corson, D. (2001) *Language, Diversity and Education*. Mahwah, NJ: Erlbaum.
Cowie, C. (2007) The accents of outsourcing: The meanings of 'neutral' in the Indian call centre industry. *World Englishes* 26, 316–330.
Cross, R. (2009) Literacy for all: Quality language education for few. *Language and Education* 23 (6), 509–522.
Day, C. (2007) School reform and transitions in teacher professionalism and identity. In T. Townsend and R. Bates (eds) *Handbook of Teacher Education: Globalization, Standards and Professionalism in Times of Change*. Dordrecht: Springer.
Dunn, K. M., Klocker, N. and Salabay, T. (2007) Contemporary racism and Islamaphobia in Australia: Racializing religion. *Ethnicities* 7 (4), 564–589.

Fleming, D. (2007) Adult ESL programs in Canada: Emerging trends in the contexts of history, economics, and identity. In J. Cummins and C. Davison (eds) *International Handbook of English Language Teaching* (Vol. 1, pp. 187–198). Norwell, MA: Springer Publishers.

Forrest, J. and Dunn, K. (2006) 'Core' culture, hegemony and multiculturalism: Perceptions of the privileged position of Australians with British backgrounds. *Ethnicities* 6 (2), 203–230.

Fraser, N. (1997) *Justice Interruptus: Critical Reflections on the 'Postsocialist' Condition*. New York: Routledge.

Gee, J.P. (2004) Learning languages as a matter of learning social languages within discourses. In M. Hawkins (ed.) *Language Learning and Teacher Education: A Sociocultural Approach* (pp. 13–31). Clevedon: Multilingual Matters.

Gibb, T.L. (2008) Bridging Canadian adult second language education and essential skills policies: Approach with caution. *Adult Education Quarterly* 58, 318–334.

Gillard, J. (2009) *Accountable Government, Accountable Communities: The Role of Transparency in Education Reform*. Brisbane: Speech to the Eidos Institute.

Grimmett, P.P., Fleming, R. and Trotter, L. (2009) Legitimacy and identity in teacher education: A micro-political struggle constrained by macro-political pressures. *Asia-Pacific Journal of Teacher Education* 37 (1), 5–26.

Gunzenhauser, M.G. (2008) Care of the self in a context of accountability. *Teachers College Record* 110 (10), 2224–2244.

Hall, H. (2009) Tensions, ironies, and social justice in black civil rights: Lessons from Brown and King. In W. Ayers, T. Quinn and D. Stovall (eds) *Handbook of Social Justice in Education*. New York: Routledge.

Haque, E. and Cray, E. (2007) Constraining teachers: Adult ESL settlement language training policy and implementation. *TESOL Quarterly* 41, 634–642.

Harvey, S. (2006) Discourses of (non) western subjectivity and philosophical recovery. *Journal of Multicultural Discourses* 1 (1), 27–34.

Hattam, R., Prosser, B. and Brady, K. (2009) Revolution or backlash? The mediatisation of education policy in Australia. *Critical Studies in Education* 50 (2), 159–172.

Hill, D. (2007) Critical teacher education, new labour, and the global project of neoliberal capital. *Policy Futures in Education* 5 (2), 204–225.

Holborow, M. (2007) Language, ideology and neoliberalism. *Journal of Language and Politics* 6 (1), 51–73.

Johnson, D., Johnson, B., Farenga, S. and Ness, D. (2005) *Trivializing Teacher Education: The Accreditation Squeeze*. Lanham, MD: Rowman & Littlefield.

Jordao, C. (2009) English as a foreign language, globalisation and conceptual questioning. *Globalisation, Societies and Education* 7 (1), 95–107.

Kamp, A. and Mansouri, F. (2009) Constructing inclusive education in a neoliberal context: Promoting inclusion of Arab-Australian students in an Australian context. *British Educational Research Journal* 99999 (1), 1–12.

Kenway, J. and Hickey-Moody, A. (2009) Moving abjection. In W. Ayers, T. Quinn and D. Stovall (eds) *Handbook of Social Justice in Education*. New York: Routledge.

Keung, N. (2007) Teacher wins 13-year bias case. *Toronto Star Newspaper*, 13 January, p. A9.

Kumaravadivelu, B. (2003) *Beyond Methods: Macrostrategies for Language Teaching*. New Haven, CT: Yale University Press.

Lake, M. and Reynolds, H. (2008) *Drawing the Global Colour Line: White Men's Countries and the Question of Racial Equality*. Cambridge: Cambridge University Press.

Liddicoat, A.J. (2009) Evolving ideologies of the intercultural in Australian multicultural and language education policy. *Journal of Multilingual and Multicultural Development*, 30 (3), 1897–203.

Leonardo, Z. (2009) Reading whiteness: Antiracist pedagogy against white racial knowledge. In W. Ayers, T. Quinn and D. Stovall (eds) *Handbook of Social Justice in Education*. New York: Routledge.

Lewington, J. (2009) Minorities missing out on top jobs: Study. *Globe and Mail Newspaper [Toronto]*, 28 May, p. A12.

Luke, A. (2006) Teaching after the market. In L. Weis, C. McCarthy and G. Dimitriadis (eds) *Ideology, Curriculum, and the New Sociology of Education: Revisiting the Work of Michael Apple* (pp. 115–141). New York: Routledge.

Luke, A., Luke, C. and Graham, P. (2007) Globalization, corporatism, and critical language education. *International Multilingual Research Journal* 1 (1), 1–13.

Lynn, M. and Smith-Maddox, R. (2007) Preservice teacher inquiry: Creating a space to dialogue about becoming a social justice educator. *Teaching and Teacher Education* 23 (1), 94–105.

Mansouri, F. and Wood, S. (2008) *Identity, Education and Belonging: Arab and Muslim Youth in Contemporary Australia*. Melbourne: Melbourne University Press.

Marginson, S. (2006) Engaging democratic education in the neoliberal age. *Educational Theory* 56 (2), 205–219.

Matthews, J. (2008) Schooling and settlement: Refugee education in Australia. *International Studies in Sociology of Education* 18 (1), 31–45.

McDonald, M. and Zeichner, K. (2009) Social justice teacher education. In W. Ayers, T. Quinn and D. Stovall (eds) *Handbook of Social Justice in Education* (pp. 595–610). New York: Routledge.

Michell, M. (1999) 'Wither' ESL? Post-literacy prospects for English as a Second Language programs in Australian schools. *Prospect* 14 (2), 4–23.

Michell, M. (2009) Implications of the national education reform agenda for migrant and refugee English as a second language learners in Australian schools. Paper presented at the National Symposium on Assessing English as a second/other language in the Australian context. Sydney, NSW.

Mills, C. (2006) Pre-service teacher education and the development of socially just dispositions: A review of the literature. Paper presented at the Australian Association for Research in Education.

Mills, C. and Ballantyne, J. (2009) Pre-service teachers' dispositions towards diversity: Arguing for a developmental hierarchy of change. *Teaching and Teacher Education* 26, 447–454.

Mills, K. (2008) Will large-scale assessments raise literacy standards in Australian schools? *Australian Journal of Language and Literacy* 31 (3), 211–225.

Morgan, B. (1987) Three dreams of language; or, no longer immured in the Bastille of the humanist word. *College English* 49, 449–458.

Morgan, B. (2009) Fostering transformative practitioners for critical EAP: Possibilities and challenges. *Journal of English for Academic Purposes* 8, 86–99.

Morgan, B. and Fleming, D. (2009) Critical citizenship practices in ESP and ESL programs: Canadian and global perspectives. In D. Belcher (ed.) *English for Specific Purposes in Theory and Practice* (pp. 264–288). Ann Arbor, MI: University of Michigan Press.

Morgan, B. and Vandrick, S. (2009) Imagining a peace curriculum: What second language education brings to the table. *Peace & Change: A Journal of Peace Research* 34, 510–532.

Ninnes, P. (2009) Language matters: Analysing curriculum materials for social justice. In I. Soliman (ed.) *Interrogating Common Sense: Teaching for Social Justice* (pp. 99–109). Frenchs Forest, NSW: Pearson.

Olssen, M., Codd, J. and O'Neill, A-M. (2004) *Education Policy: Globalization, Citizenship and Democracy.* London: Sage.

Owen, M. and Nason, D. (2009) Indigenous kids better off in jail: South Australian A-G Michael Atkinson. *The Australian*, 13 October, pp. 1–2. On WWW at http://www.theaustralian.com.au/news/indigenous-kids-better-off-in-jail-south-australian-a-g-michael-atkinson/story-e6frg6p6-1225786083208. Accessed October 2009.

Palmer, H. (1976) Mosaic versus melting pot? Immigration and ethnicity in Canada and the United States. *International Journal* 31, 488–528.

Pennycook, A. (1994) English in the world/the world in English. In J. Tollefson (ed.) *Power and Inequality in Language Education* (pp. 34–58). Cambridge: Cambridge University Press.

Phillipson, R. (2008) The linguistic imperialism of neoliberal empire. *Critical Inquiry in Language Studies* 5 (1), 1–43.

Pinet, R. (2006) The contestation of citizenship education at three stages of the LINC 4 & 5 curriculum guidelines: Production, reception, and implementation. *TESL Canada Journal* 24 (1), 1–21.

Ramanathan, V. and Morgan, B. (2009) Global warning? West-based TESOL, class-blindness and the challenge for critical pedagogies. In F. Sharifian (ed.) *English as an International Language: Perspectives and Pedagogical Issues* (pp. 153–168). Bristol: Multilingual Matters.

Reagan, T. (2004) Objectification, positivism and language studies: A reconsideration. *Critical Inquiry in Language Studies* 1 (1), 41–60.

Santoro, N. and Allard, A. (2005) (Re)examining identities: Working with diversity in the pre-service teaching experience. *Teaching and Teacher Education* 21 (7), 863–873.

Sleeter, C. (2007) *Facing Accountability in Education: Democracy and Equity at Risk.* New York: Teachers College Press.

Soliman, I. (ed.) (2009) *Interrogating Common Sense: Teaching for Social Justice.* Frenchs Forest, NSW: Pearson.

Steger, M.B. (2003) *Globalization: A Very Short Introduction.* Oxford: Oxford University Press.

Talbert-Johnson, C. (2006) Preparing highly qualified teacher candidates for urban schools: The importance of dispositions. *Education and Urban Society* 39 (1), 147–160.

Thomson, R.I. and Derwing, T.M. (2004) Presenting Canadian values in LINC: The roles of textbooks and teachers. *TESL Canada Journal* 21 (2), 17–33.

van Lier, L. (2004) *The Ecology and Semiotics of Language Learning: A Sociocultural Perspective.* Dordrecht: Kluwer.

Villegas, A. (2007) Dispositions in teacher education: A look at social justice. *Journal of Teacher Education* 58 (5), 370–380.

Warnock, J.W. (2004) *Saskatchewan: The Roots of Discontent and Protest*. Montreal: Black Rose Books.

Welch, A. (2007) Cultural difference and identity. In R. Connell, C. Campbell, M. Vickers, A. Welch, D. Foley and N. Bagnall (eds) *Education, Change and Society* (pp. 155–187). New York: Oxford University Press.

Williams, C.H. (1998) Introduction: Representing the citizens – reflections on language policy in Canada and the United States. In T. Ricento and B. Burnaby (eds) *Language and Politics in the United States and Canada* (pp. 1–32). Mahwah, NJ: Erlbaum.

Chapter 5

Enfranchising the Teacher of English through Action Research: Perspectives on English Language Teacher Education in Uganda

ROBINAH KYEYUNE

Introduction

Reflection on social justice in language teacher education should make reference to the learners' need to function as able and active members of their social groups and to the burden that teacher trainers must carry for equipping teachers to satisfy these needs. Part of the teacher trainers' accountability is taking stock of specific language teacher education practices and their strengths and weaknesses. English being a second and official language in Uganda, as well as a compulsory school subject and the dominant medium of instruction, its teachers occupy a central place in curriculum implementation. We need therefore to reflect on the contribution that we can make to social justice teacher education, primarily by evaluating our approach to the preparation of teachers of English. This chapter argues that we should train teachers in action research skills to empower them to work as curriculum leaders who not only understand the varied needs of their learners but also respond to them creatively and satisfactorily and with professional authority. Thus, confident in their tested knowledge and techniques, the teachers should be effective and constantly cause improvement in the learners' language abilities and their own confidence to participate in social dialogue. The chapter starts with a review of Uganda's education system and language education policy, against which background the teacher training programs are criticized for equipping teachers with theoretical knowledge and inadequate professional skills. It goes on to describe the disenfranchisement of teachers and learners that results from this imbalance, explaining how the teacher's lack of professional authority leads, in turn, to learners' lack of functional language abilities. It then recommends cultivation of a culture of critical inquiry and action research by teacher trainers and teachers, and the constant review of gaps in knowledge and teaching practices as means to improvement of teacher training and teaching, respectively.

Language in Society and Education in Uganda

Uganda's education context is characterized by a multiplicity of learners' and teachers' language backgrounds and the elevated status of English in society and in education in particular. The significance of these and other elements hangs on the interplay of language, English language teaching and language teacher education issues in the education context described here.

Uganda has a pyramidal education system that is made up of three major levels. Normal progress through these levels spans an average of 16 years. The primary level, which a child enters at an average age of six years, lasts seven years. Secondary education lasts six years after which the individual joins college or university and graduates after three to six years depending on the program of study that he or she chooses to follow. Some children, especially in the metropolitan areas, join primary education after privileged exposure to nursery and preprimary education. There are many more beneficiaries at the lower grades of this education system, with the number thinning more and more higher up in the system. With the implementation of the universal primary education program from 1997, opening up educational access to millions of previously excluded children, enrolment rose from 2.7 million in 1996 to 7.3 million in 2007. This development in the primary subsector led to a bulge in access to secondary education and, although no definite secondary enrolment figures are available, the rising secondary enrolment means an increased number of beneficiaries who need English.

There are 43 living local languages altogether in Uganda, some with fully developed orthographies and some spoken by large groups while others are used by much smaller groups. They are grouped under collective labels related to ethnic groupings, which are themselves identified with regional divisions. In the central, southern, eastern and western regions, the people speak *Bantu* languages, among which Luganda, Runyankore-Rukiga, Runyoro-Rutooro, Lusoga and Lumasaba are designated major local languages. Luo is spoken in the northern region, and is among the country's major local languages. Ḍakarimajong, the language of the Karamoja region in the northeast, is also a recognized major language. In the northwestern region, the different groups speak several languages among which Lugbara is a major Ugandan language. Another major language, Ateso, is spoken in the far eastern subregion.

Outside the home, local languages are spoken in places of worship and in community meetings. They are the medium of mass mobilization activities, while the major languages are also the medium of some print and broadcast media programs. Local languages are very significant in education. The national language education policy specifies the local language or mother tongue as the language of instruction (LOI) in the first three years of primary school, in acknowledgment of the fundamental place of the child's language in the functions of conceptualization and in the learning process. At this level, English is taught as a subject. The policy, contained in the 1992 Education White Paper and based principally on the report of the Education Review Commission (1989), represents a return to the language education practices of the 50s and 60s. It affirms the cognitive needs and linguistic rights of the child, asserting overall the place of language in equitable provision of education for the masses.

However, a few factors combine to undermine the status of local languages in education. There is a common perception of English as a source of prestige and the surest route to educational excellence and work opportunities at home and abroad. There is also a lack of supervision of implementation and the competition for grades in the primary leaving examination, which is administered in English. Also the allowance for urban schools to use English at lower primary to cater to their multiethnic multilingual population weakens the LOI implementation. On the other hand, this allowance illustrates that English is perceived as a common language that can be instrumental in closing the communication gaps between native speakers of different local languages.

English is a second and official language in Uganda and the lingua franca of trade and industry, law, commerce, religion and politics, as well as the predominant language of dissemination of public literature and mass media. Messages about, say, malaria, HIV/AIDS and tuberculosis; education; taxes; water and sanitation and other development issues are disseminated in English and translated into the major local languages. More significantly, English is the LOI in upper primary school – Primary Four to Seven, where pupils are 9–13 years old on average. At this level, children also learn it as a subject. It is also the LOI and a compulsory subject at secondary school, where students are on average 13–18 years old, as well as the LOI in higher education. English proficiency is, however, expected only among those who have had formal schooling. Perhaps for this reason, the language assumes a prestigious position. Going to school, sometimes mistaken for being educated, is often equated with being able to speak good English. In comparison, European languages in the curriculum, including French, Latin and German, are accorded the status of 'foreign languages', which is secondary to that of second language.

In the current secondary curriculum of eight subject categories, which are also reflected in the examination syllabus (Uganda National Examinations Board), English Language is a subject as well as a category. The other subjects fall into seven categories, as shown in the table below. This categorization illustrates the status of English in education.

Subject Categorization

Subject category	Subjects
I English Language	English Language
II Humanities	Literature in English, Fasihi ya Kiswahili, Christian Religious Education (Christian Living Today), Christian Religious Education (with traditional African religions), Islamic Religious Education, History, Geography, Political Education
III Languages	Latin, German, French, Luganda, Lugha ya Kiswahili, Arabic
IV Mathematics	Mathematics, Additional Mathematics
V Science	General Science, Agriculture: Principles and Practices, Physics, Chemistry, Biology
VI Cultural and Others	Art, Music, Health Education, Clothing and Textiles, Foods and Nutrition, Home Management
VII Technical	Woodwork, Technical Drawing, Metalwork, Building Construction, Electricity and Electronics, Power and Energy
VIII Business	Commerce, Principles of Accounts, Shorthand, Typewriting, Office Practice, Computer Studies, Entrepreneurship Skills

The objectives of examining English Language illustrate the pedagogical principles behind its inclusion in the examination syllabus – Uganda National Examinations Board views it as a subject as well as a medium of communication. The examination objectives are as follows:

(1) To develop the student's ability to understand and use current English for effective communication, and
(2) To widen the student's knowledge and active and effective communication of English through exposure to writing in English of various kinds. (Uganda National Examinations Board).

English is given further importance by its inclusion among the seven core subjects (out of the proposed total of 10) in the framework of support in the universal secondary education program. In this framework, it is recognized as a critical tool of communication both at school and in life in general. According to an appraisal of the secondary subsector (Ministry of Education and Sports, 2008), English 'gives the learner the basis for communicating and analysing issues using appropriate language' and '... it helps in developing of the skill of reading widely, a skill that is needed across the curriculum'. English is therefore considered a major tool of learning in the curriculum. This signifies a public and official awareness of and sympathy with the language across the curriculum principle. The status of English implies that teachers' and learners' mastery of the language is a prerequisite to the latters' benefiting from instruction and to their knowledge and ability being passed as relevant as well as current. It endorses our responsibility for reviewing language teacher education programs for their value. We shall return to these implications presently with regard to the targets of our programs.

Teacher Preparation Targets versus Social Demands

There has been a long-standing belief that what teachers of English need to be equipped with is the ability to teach the young people in school how to speak and write correct English in appropriate expressions and to read and listen with understanding. Thus, our undergraduate teacher training programs are led by general objectives such as equipping the learner with the knowledge and skills required for them to help students improve their knowledge and use of English. Often, we describe the effective teacher as one who ably organizes learning activities that support the mastery of language skills as is demonstrable in learners' fluent use of English in life-like situations.

It must be convenient to keep such a general view of responsibility for language learning and use. It helps minimize any concerns for individual learners' needs, and consequently makes secondary any awareness of the need for providing language learning resources. Thanks to the politics of program and course ownership, our university academic programs produce teachers with in-depth knowledge of linguistics that they cannot use to equip students with the competences that society demands. Teachers can illustrate numerous derivations in the grammar of English but possess very little pedagogic and professional capital. They cannot align their knowledge with their learner's language needs and make decisions of how best to help them improve their listening, reading, writing or speaking abilities. Faced with an assessment system that emphasizes grades, the teachers find themselves torn between the principles of a good teacher who should enable the learner to connect with self, others and the world (Liston *et al.*, 2008) and the expectations of a qualified teacher whose abilities should be reflected in the learners' examination performance.

Often newly qualified teachers of English may demonstrate sensitivity to individual learners' abilities and weaknesses and organize learning activities that expose learners to simulated acquisition-rich situations. They are keen to organize drama, debate, writing and other activities and offer genuine feedback on performance. But as they gain experience and make sense of their work environment, they soon lose confidence in their own efforts when they cannot determine how to meet the specific learning needs. And this is especially because the system demands good grades from everyone and does not cater to individuals. The teachers resort to the routines prescribed by the examination syllabus, anxious to identify with their immediate social groups in the schools that evaluate them. They feed students on the discrete grammar of English, composition writing in the form of creative writing and reading comprehension without much care for the functional approach. In their role as curriculum implementers, many teachers of English work with the frustration of subscribing to the standardized management paradigm in which, according to Henderson and Gornik (2007), the actors pursue standards regardless of the means by which they are obtained.

Teachers generally have little capacity to do much else. The initial teacher preparation program consists of English Language Studies, which is basically linguistics and literature. It equips teacher trainees with knowledge of linguistics and literature taught as Arts disciplines in a university unit removed from the one that deals in preparing teaching professionals. The teacher trainees are taught the theories of language acquisition and learning, the phonetics and phonology of English, the morphology of English, the syntax of English, stylistics, discourse analysis, varieties of English and comparative linguistics by faculty specialized in these content areas of English Language Studies. They learn literary theory, oral literature, East African literature, the short story, poetry, the novel and drama by another set of expert faculty. Education courses, which dwell on methodological and professional content, occupy only 84 hours or 3.9% of the 2160 hours allocated to the teaching subjects – in this case English Language Teaching (ELT) and Literature. The hours allocated to teaching subjects are spread over the last three semesters in a six-semester program. In these courses the trainees are taught the place of language in literature teaching; how to teach the different literary genres; how to develop materials for literature classes; how to teach the various language skills and how to plan teaching. For practicum, the trainees engage in 12 weeks of school practice twice during the program, once at the end of the fourth semester and the second time at the end of the sixth semester. This aspect of training is part of a qualification examination and is supervised by faculty and hired staff who go into the schools, assess classroom lessons and report in a structured document that specifies various areas of interest including the lesson plan, lesson objectives, lesson content and lesson delivery. This training scenario presents significant disproportions – a distinct bias for theoretical content knowledge that caters to a mastery of linguistics; neglect of pedagogical content knowledge and pedagogical skills and a distance between English teacher trainees and language education faculty. The distance between language education specialist and trainee means that the prospective teacher of English is bound to complete the training program without optimal exposure to contexts that would guide and support his or her development of professional skills.

In my view there is no commitment to the understanding of pedagogy and the development of pedagogical skills. Evidently we too find no excitement in training teachers of English, and respond to the requirements in our job without any enthusiasm for continuing to learn about language development or about language learning and use. The most significant outcome of this is the teachers' limited understanding of the constant change in the use of English and in the learners' expectations for their teachers' guidance. They thus join teaching as misfits in what Eraut (1985) describes as the complexity of the education process, characterized by unstable conditions that dictate that teachers are the best evaluators of the problems therein, being more knowledgeable about the conditions than the rest of society is. Thus held back, the teachers cannot claim ownership of their experience and, without the required agency, they conduct teaching without conviction of the individual and social learning needs surrounding English teaching. Without this conviction, as Henderson and Kesson (2004) argue, they cannot cause change. And yet, citing Smyth (1987), Woods (1989) observes that teachers are expected to effect social change through impacting the social and intellectual development of young people.

Disenfranchised Teachers and Learners

In spite of the provision of a secondary English syllabus that presents a selection of language content and a suggestion of how it should be taught, teachers often come back to the university to consult on how to teach various aspects of English. Their common areas of concern include spelling, correct sentence construction, vocabulary, writing interestingly and correctly, note-making, inference and logical presentation of thought and poetry. In spite of the revelation that they do not know about the existence of the syllabus, these inquiries provide useful clues to the teachers' awareness. At one level, teachers are aware of their responsibility for assessing the learner's needs and for matching these with the selection and application of specific teaching approaches and techniques. Yet, they acknowledge their lack of the skills required to teach the cited aspects of language use. Besides, the teachers demonstrate awareness of the learners' potential to learn and use language in domains well beyond those that may be illustrated in the syllabus. At another level, they are aware of their own lack of the professional authority required for them to determine the most appropriate approach to solving the recognized problems.

Clearly, then, there are significant gaps in the profile of the teachers of English that our teacher preparation programs produce. The pedagogic implications cited earlier therefore assume a democratic value as well. They point to the possible variations in the English language content taught in schools besides variations in pedagogical and personal approaches and in learning effectiveness. The variations imply inclusion of learners who have enjoyed adequate exposure to good models of English in primary school and have achieved a reasonable level of mastery of English by the time they join secondary school, which may continue to develop through secondary school. On the other hand, they threaten exclusion of learners previously exposed to poor models or insufficient amounts of the language, whose development of English language competences is bound to be less than satisfactory. This inequity works against the positive development of increased access to secondary education. Since the latter category are most likely from disadvantaged backgrounds, they experience a complex set of inequities that work either to force them out of school altogether or to delay their completion of the cycle. Such inequitable outcomes of the teaching of English place not only the learner, the object of change, but also the teacher, the agent of change, at a disadvantage. I find it useful to view the teacher and learner as groups whose rights have been infringed upon. This view guides my examination in the rest of this section.

As long as they consult about how to teach English, teachers demonstrate their capacity to critique their situation for its demands on their competences. Besides, they help us evaluate our programs and our performance as teacher trainers. While it is true that there are gaps in the syllabus as well, I want to suggest that for now, our reflection invests in a focus on the teacher and the teacher trainer. The teachers' behavior illustrates the control that we retain over them and over the process of learning, as well as the control that we wield over the use of English. If they had the knowledge, confidence and professionalism required to resolve their needs, the teachers would creatively manipulate the syllabus and other resources in their environment to enable their learners to master English vocabulary, spell better and write more interesting text among other improvements. This way they would fit Liston *et al.*'s (2008) description of effective teachers and their trainers who, besides integrating subject knowledge and skills, possess the confidence to apply these creatively and to engage in critical reflection on their practice as certain means to improvement.

That they are unable to make decisions regarding the situations that they know best illustrates a significant lack of authority. It points to a power imbalance in which we, the trainers, refuse to add to the training program a component that would cater to confidence building and decision making. In maintaining the position of *trainer* and at the same time retaining the authority of *advisor* on the teacher's context, we unjustly exercise a power over the classroom learning process in situations far removed from us, which we hardly understand. Such a custodial relationship between trainer and trained is a significant form of social dominance, characterized mainly by deception. The teachers leave the training program at the university believing that their linguistic knowledge places them at a social advantage only to have the real world prove to them that the real possession in this world is professional influence. This social dominance is further embodied in the fact that the teachers, who are the majority, occupy the position of uninformed doers while the trainers, who are the minority, keep the formidable position of passive knowers. Both groups may be quite unaware of the nuances of this relationship, for neither group intends their behavior. However, critical reflection requires that we expose this power imbalance: enjoyment of a privileged social position by the minority while the majority are deprived of the consciousness that is prerequisite to action for changing their own situation.

Exposition of this power imbalance is useful for unearthing a fundamental cause for the lack of excitement that seems to characterize the lives of teachers of English. The tendency for them to perform routines of teaching grammar, comprehension, summary and composition may arise from the teachers' realization that our advice does not ease the challenges of their work. Brindley's (1994) assertion on teaching English assumes specific relevance for our reflection. He points out that English meets new challenges, given the multiplicity of needs that manifest every day, which translate into demands for teachers to update their subject knowledge. And he describes this very condition as the source of excitement. The observation suggests that rather than continuously rushing to solicit the trainer's advice on the challenges in the teaching context, the teacher should be stimulated to respond on the basis of personal judgments. In particular he or she should endeavor to learn more about the language and about English language pedagogy than he or she was taught in the teacher preparation program and go on to apply and later evaluate the pedagogy for effectiveness. Adequately and appropriately excited about the challenges, an effective teacher of English should discuss his or her evaluation essentially as an evaluation of the training program. Such a teacher would align his or her work with Brindley's (1994) assessment of the requirements of teaching English:

> The work of teaching English involves continual progressing for the expression of alternative ideas, inviting challenge to received opinions, seeking strong personal responses, establishing debate. (Brindley, 1994: 11)

Views of the teacher as a judge are reinforced by Dickinson's (2010) assertion on the teacher's entitlement to freedom to make decisions about his or her learners' needs and identify suitable resources with regard to the learners' needs and environment. Dickinson argues that the teacher should enjoy the '... autonomy in selecting what is appropriate, adding to it and shaping the materials for the particular class's needs and circumstances as well as the individual within each class'. However, the training background that does not equip them to critique received knowledge and the school system that does not encourage individual excellence deprive the teachers of that kind of personal authority.

Since our teachers find no excitement in their work, in spite of the challenges that they acknowledge, we must act against the power imbalance to ensure the possibility of excitement and teachers' capacity for transacting agency. We need to resist the temptation of advising about methods of teaching in a context that we do not understand and seek, rather, to enable teachers to analyze and evaluate that context through committed inquiry for decision making. We shall return to details of this presently. Here the emphasis is that in appreciating the lack of excitement for teachers of English we in fact accept a criticism that the objectives of our teacher preparation program are not appropriate for the teaching context. Teachers are challenged to respond to the questions of young adults who enjoy unstructured exposure to various models such as are discernible in television, cinema, novels and magazines and other colorful media. The learners quickly learn from these sources of language that appeal to them, especially by endorsing their identity as members of specific social groups. Emulating these social groups, they learn English by using it in very dynamic ways. On the other hand, the teachers attempt to teach them English by ways that moderate their experiences and make the language a subject rather than a resource in expression. The learners therefore reject the teachers' approaches, causing erosion rather than boosting of the latters' confidence.

If teachers had a sound knowledge of the Input Hypothesis (Krashen, 1985), they would be better positioned to find a solution nearer home, and would have control over any options for action. Their search for answers far beyond the local context is evidence of a lack not only of theoretical knowledge requisite to effective teaching but also of a professional understanding of the changes in English and our use of it. Knowledge of these changes is argued by Wyse and Jones (2001) to be central to success in teaching. The teacher should be able to debate the comprehensible input that the learners should be exposed to in search of improvement and present not only meaningful but also exciting tasks that end in language learning. As an authority over the learning process, the teacher should also be able to judge the learners' progression along the acquisition scale, thereby evaluating his or her own efforts for input and the learners' response to input.

Demand for Critical Inquiry by Trainers

Evaluation of the efficacy of the training programs that produce teachers of English is incomplete without a judgment of the trainer's achievement. And this judgment should be performed by us, in search of answers to questions about the value of our practices. It consists in praxis as advocated by, say, Lather (1991) by which education practice we make a genuine effort to critique the status quo in search of a just society. Praxis in the context of training teachers of English should facilitate democracy in our programs by adding to them the demand for our overt evaluation of their functionality.

A series of questions is in order, then, as part of the process of inquiry. What is the profile of the teacher of English that we should send out into the world? What content knowledge and pedagogical content knowledge do teachers of English need to be able to align to the actual current demands for use of English in school and in the world of work? What pedagogical skills do teachers need to transfer the knowledge and skills of English that are demanded by the students and those who will evaluate them after school? What professional authority is required of teachers of English in their work in school? Beyond these we should ask where all the knowledge occurs and how the teachers can access and understand it, thus reflecting on power and authority issues. We should be well guided by Rodgers' (2002) description of reflective practice. Rodgers identifies four key characteristics of reflective practice that, in my view, the teacher trainer should recognize. The language teacher trainer and the English teacher trainee both make meaning of their experience through connections to others, which makes reflective practice a must for them. Their interaction should be a source of learning rather than a means of the trainer's imposition of unjust influence on the trainee. Being a part of systematic community interaction would place them in sync with the problems that they are expected to solve and enable both to critique these with informed and unbiased judgment. Lastly, they should use reflection in search of personal and intellectual growth of oneself and others, which would make the relationship between teacher and trainer one of support rather than of dominance.

As trainers our lack of growth renders wasteful the teachers' trust in our abilities, since our authority does not empower them to maximize the gains of their experience. Without any conviction on goals for our own personal and intellectual growth, we cannot be fully committed to supporting newly qualified teachers' endeavors for enabling learners to master English and learn effectively. We therefore cannot contribute to their social development and that of the young people whose learning is entrusted in their hands. By this inadequacy we contribute to the building of a socially unjust world in which young people cannot achieve their potential or be active and confident participants in their social setting. For correction I advocate democratic inquiry based on what is described as democratic self- and social understanding by Henderson and Gornik (2007). This should be blended with knowledge of problem-solving approaches in the design of staff development programs for increasing the teacher trainer's capacity to support the teacher's intellectual and professional development. As Shor (1993) argues, this practice should enhance learning for both the trainer and the teacher. Teachers can be better able to make informed decisions about their work and its demands, thus lessening the social imbalance earlier noted. It is necessary that reflective practice and problem solving starts during teacher training programs as a lived culture shared by the trainer and the teacher trainee so that the one trains reflection and the other learns it by doing. Woodward's (1991) suggestions for teacher training models premised on theories of learning by doing are useful in this regard. Having learnt in a hands-on approach, the teachers would be well positioned to practice inquiry after training. They would also position themselves at the center, rather than depend on the teacher trainers to play center stage singly.

Training Teachers in Action Research

Appreciating the gaps in language teacher training gives specific significance to investment in action research during the training programs. Although teachers are unable to make some crucial decisions in their work, their consultation illustrates sensitivity to the conditions in their work environment. It offers us an opportunity to grow a culture of reflective inquiry that Henderson and Gornik (2007) encourage for curriculum leadership but that is missing in our programs. To ensure fairness in the evaluation of teachers' performance, we ought to integrate action research and reflective inquiry courses in the English language teacher training programs as a means of empowering teachers to effect change. To do this well we need to spell out some crucial components of such courses. Some recommendations are explained in this section.

Action research training should aim at enabling teachers to practice inquiry as input into deliberate choice for, say, content and methodology. Recognizing the value of praxis, at the global level we should structure the training program into a sandwich mode that provides for a three-tier approach. In the first year, following a brief initial exposure to the aims of language teaching and the place of language in society, particularly English in this case, the trainee should be placed in school as a teaching practitioner with a researcher role. This should be followed by theory-based teaching at the university to review the teaching experience.

A return to the school should follow in the final stage of training to test the ideas that would have been cultivated in the review. In this practice–theory–review approach, the trainer should entrench the trainee in the school as a peer in a collegial team of teachers of English who conduct reflective inquiry on the choices for their teaching approaches and methods and the effectiveness of their teaching. The trainer's responsibility involves identifying among the school teaching and administrative staff a core of colleagues, including those with proven experience and some newly qualified teachers, who will provide the required support for inquiry and meaning-making. The peers should constantly seek to identify what is unsatisfactory and share lessons about what they should change and the means of changing it.

Here is a hypothetical situation in which this requirement could be operationalized. The English language teacher trainee is required to satisfy a course requirement for identifying a specific teaching-learning issue that threatens to invalidate or make debatable his or her knowledge about language teaching and learning. The issue could relate to theories of language acquisition and development but should clearly have implications for the language teacher's and learners' roles. It may be, for example, learners' lack of English vocabulary and structures, which manifests in low levels of communicative ability in speaking. The trainee's task is to establish and document in detail not only the manifestations of the problem but also its possible sources, based on observation of experience in a specified context. I suggest a set of questions to guide teachers' understanding of the symptomatic language teaching and learning problem. Does the teacher's choice of teaching approaches and techniques have any bearing on the learners' actual ability? How does the lack relate to learners' perceptions of what is adequate and what is important? What is the place of amount of practice by learners at home and/or at school? Is the causal factor singular, or are there multiple causes? Does any of the knowledge learnt on the university course explain the occurrence? In all this the trainee is required to show his or her position – for example, observer or teacher-observer, and how this position influences what is considered important.

Elliott (1993) describes two options that trainees may reflect on for a choice of approach to change, although his expressed preference for one may easily bias the practitioner. In one option, the practitioner starts with reflection on what is unsatisfactory and then goes on to effect change. In the other, Elliott's preference, the practitioner starts with changing the way he or she teaches and then goes on to reflect on the effect of the change. Elliot describes the first option as one that is distanced and based on academic knowledge, which may render its selection akin to dependence on theory. He argues that since it depends on a thought-out solution, this choice demands a lot of time whereas the alternative allows the practitioner to explore potential solutions while at the same time evaluating their aptness to the situation.

Summary and Conclusion

In this chapter I have shown the key status of English in Uganda, which makes the training of teachers of English an important means of enabling young people to master the school curriculum, obtaining the academic grades they seek and participating in social and professional dialogue beyond the school setting. I have argued that there is a discrepancy between the heavily theoretical training of teachers at the university and the reality of language teaching demands in schools. Owing to this discrepancy, newly qualified teachers often face the challenge of satisfying the learners' quest for relevant and useful language content and skills but are usually unable to decide how to help the learners realize the goals of learning English. And lacking the requisite pedagogical skills and professional authority to inform any action, teachers turn back to us, the trainers, for solutions to the challenge, which is ironical since we know very little about their specific teaching contexts. I have argued the need to exploit this opportunity for an improvement of our English teacher training practice, recommending that action research become a key element of teacher preparation programs. The chapter encourages reflective inquiry on the power relations between teachers and teacher trainers as a means of correcting the imbalance therein. It recommends placing the teacher at the center of the training program, exploiting teachers' feedback on their training and teaching experience and using the lessons to contribute to social justice in English language teacher education.

References

Brindley, S. (ed.) (1994) *Teaching English in the Secondary School*. London: Routledge and Open University.

Dickinson, P. (2010) Developments in English. In S. Clarke, P. Dickinson and J. Westbrook (eds) *The Complete Guide to Becoming an English Teacher*. London: Sage.

Elliott, J. (1993) *Action Research for Educational Change*. Buckingham: Open University.

Eraut, M. (1985) In-service education and training of teachers. *International Encyclopaedia of Education* 2511–2526.

Henderson, J.G. and Gornik, R. (2007) *Transformative Curriculum Leadership*, (3rd edn), Upper Saddle River NJ: Pearson.

Henderson, J.G. and Kesson, K.R. (2004) *Curriculum Wisdom: Educational Decisions in Democratic Societies*. Upper Saddle River NJ: Merrill Prentice-Hall.

Krashen, J. (1985) *The Input Hypothesis: Issues and Implications*. London: Longman

Lather, P. (1991) *Getting Smart: Feminist Research and the Post-modern Pedagogy*. New York: Routledge.

Liston, D., Borko, H. and Whitcomb, J. (2008) The teacher educator's role in enhancing teacher quality. *Journal of Teacher Education* 59 (2), 111–116.

Ministry of Education and Sports, Uganda (2008) Report of pre-appraisal mission for World Bank support to universal secondary education, March 25–April 4, 2008, Aide Memoire.

Republic of Uganda (1989) *Education for National Integration and Development*. Report of the Education Review Commission. Kampala Uganda.

Rodgers, C.R. (2002) Seeing student learning. Teacher change and the role of reflection. *Harvard Educational Review* 72 (2), 230–253.

Shor, I. (1993) Education is politics: Paulo Freire's critical pedagogy. In P. MacLaren and P. Leonard (eds) *Paulo Freire: A Critical Encounter*. New York: Routledge.

Smyth, J. (1987) *Educating Teachers: Changing the Nature of Pedagogical Knowledge*. New York: Falmer Press.

Uganda National Examinations Board (2006) *Uganda Certificate of Education regulations and syllabuses 2006–2010*, Kampala.

Woods, P. (1989) *Working for Teacher Development*. Norfolk: Peter Francis Publishers.

Woodward, T. (1991) *Models and Metaphors in Language Teacher Training: Loop Input and Other Strategies*. Cambridge: Cambridge University Press.

Wyse, D. and Jones, R. (2001) *Teaching English Language and Literacy*. London: Routledge/Falmer.

Chapter 6
Dialogic Determination: Constructing a Social Justice Discourse in Language Teacher Education

MARGARET R. HAWKINS

Introduction

There is, in the United States as well as internationally, a growing concern about the impact of globalization and diversity on education, and a growing awareness that youth are not being educated, nor succeeding academically, in equal or equitable ways. There has been much research and scholarly attention to dimensions of difference – that is, that certain factors put youth more or less at risk for school failure, and these factors include race, ethnicity, socioeconomic status, proficiency in the language of instruction, transience, (dis)ability and family structure, among others. For many, this results in a language of deficiency, wherein the blame for school failure resides in students and families, and not in schools, educational systems and societal structures. In an era of increasing globalization, with ever-increasing movement of resources (including and especially people) across time and space, and ever-more-convoluted political environments, policies and societal issues and debates around immigrants, it becomes imperative that educators accept the need for change, and work to design school environments, programs, curriculum and pedagogy in ways that are responsive to and inclusive of new populations and new resources.

As Zeichner has pointed out, there are societal inequities worldwide not just in schooling, but '... in access to shelter, food, healthcare, transportation, access to meaningful work that pays a living wage ...' (Zeichner, this volume: 7). These are linked to education not only in correspondence (i.e. the same youth and families who receive substandard education are likely to have substandard shelter, food, healthcare etc.) but also causally, in that a cycle is created whereby undereducated youth have less opportunity for adequate employment, leading to lack of adequate healthcare, shelter, food and so on. And lack of shelter, food, healthcare and transportation may impede school attendance and performance. In addition, anti-immigrant sentiment and policies affect school and community environments, ultimately serving to impede school attendance and success. Thus, education is deeply linked to social systems, and a stand-alone approach to 'fixing' schools is unlikely to effect substantive change. This has been recognized in fields related to health and healthcare, agriculture, economy and so on as they address issues of change in the developing world; the current turn is to integrated, cross-disciplinary approaches to sustainable change. Thus, added to already-overburdened schools and teachers is the need to understand the societal and community structures within which schools and families are embedded, to see how they are linked to education and to life possibilities, and to work to effect change not just at the individual level but also at the societal level. This is a very tall order.

In the United States, while there has been a long history of immigration, issues attendant to immigrants have been largely focused on what has been termed 'gateway communities'. These are the large urban areas where immigrants have historically settled. A newer phenomenon is the increasing number of immigrants and refugees settling in nongateway communities; smaller towns and rural areas have recently increasingly seen influxes of (often poor) immigrant and refugee families, especially in the Midwest and southeast regions of the country (Levinson *et al.*, 2007). Thus, there is an argument that *all* teachers (and school administrators) must be prepared to teach students from 'other' language and cultural backgrounds, as it is now inconceivable that teachers in virtually any region of the country will not, in the span of their teaching practice, teach culturally and linguistically diverse students. In this chapter, I explore a graduate-level university program for already-licensed and practicing K–12 teachers that offers an add-on credential for teaching English learners. The program adopts a social justice perspective, but there are, as you will see, inherent tensions and difficulties in concretizing and implementing such an approach.

Educating English Learners

While there is relative consensus in the academic literature and, increasingly, in educational policy in the United States that all teachers must be prepared to teach English learners, there is no commensurate consensus about what appropriate and adequate preparation is. There are, in effect, two distinct schools of thought in literature and resources pertaining to teacher education: one that focuses on teachers' knowledge about language forms, features, fields and functions; and another that focuses on teachers' abilities to teach in culturally and linguistically responsive ways. While theories of language often include both – and indeed I suspect that there are not many applied linguists who would claim that only grammar, or only social and cultural issues, matter – nonetheless in the past decade or so, as literature and industry within the field of education around educating English learners has proliferated, a theory of grammar as inextricably tied to register within social/political spheres is not visible.

Those who consider issues of language call for teachers to learn about grammatical structures, language functions, the four domains of language (reading, writing, listening and speaking), unpacking the language demands of texts and activities, disciplinary-specific forms of language and so on (e.g. Dutro & Moran, 2003; Echevarria *et al.*, 2006; Schleppegrell, 2004; WIDA Consortium, 2007; Wong Fillmore & Snow, 2000). Those who focus on culturally and linguistically responsive pedagogies attend to the inequities between what learners bring to school and what they need to succeed in school, how school versus out-of-school knowledge is differentially valued within schools and how to bridge such differences in equitable and caring ways. They point to

- acknowledging, valuing, recruiting and building on what students know and bring;
- focusing on effective classroom participation structures;
- engaging students in authentic collaborative tasks with appropriate scaffolding;
- connecting the worlds of home and school;
- understanding interconnections between languages, literacies, cultures and the construction of identities;
- valuing, supporting and utilizing students' home languages, and
- exploring teachers' own beliefs, attitudes and values

(De Jong & Harper, 2005; Gibbons, 2002; Gonzalez *et al.*, 2005; Hawkins, 2010; Lucas *et al.*, 2008; Richards *et al.*, Forde 2007; Valdes, 1998, 2001; Villegas & Lucas, 2007).

These two distinct bodies of literature have not, as yet, come together in an integrative fashion within discourses of teacher education, although it is reasonable to assume that both sets of components are necessary to effectively support the language, literacy and academic development of English learners. The important point for our purpose here is that while, in the current standards- and assessment-driven educational climate in the United States and elsewhere, educators in schools and districts are primarily focusing on the first (language-specific) set of competencies and knowledge indicators (as those represent the aspects of language competence that are readily measurable and are, indeed, measured), the second (culturally and linguistically responsive) set is a necessary component of social justice language teacher education. One question that arises is whether in fact it is not only necessary but also sufficient (when combined with attention to forms and features of language): what is the difference between culturally and linguistically responsive practice, and social justice practice?

Social Justice Language Teacher Education

Zeichner (this volume) points to terminology currently in use in teacher education, such as 'social reconstructionist teacher education, anti-racist teacher education, critical teacher education and social reconstructionist multicultural teacher education', claiming that these terms have similar meanings, but arguing for the ascendency of the term 'social justice teacher education' (Zeichner, this volume: 7). He claims that 'the social justice agenda ... incorporates various aspects of what has been referred to as social reconstructionist, multicultural, antiracist, bilingual, and inclusive education' (Zeichner, this volume: 10).

Similar terminological tensions have occurred within the field of language teacher education, as language teacher educators have called for first a 'sociocultural approach' and then a 'critical approach' to language teacher education (Hawkins & Norton, 2009). As is always true with labels, new concepts call for labels to identify them and, once identified, they become contested terrain among various groups of people who use them to connote different (although sometimes similar) meanings. The labels themselves become imbued with meanings ascribed to them by the communities of people who use them, and are thus tied to their historical usages. Thus, while 'critical language teacher education' certainly encompasses and even implies a need for social justice work, it has come to signify language teacher education practices that pay overt attention to issues of power as they relate to race, class, culture and language, and to the need to make these issues visible in practice. Once again, this is a necessary but perhaps not sufficient component of social justice language teacher education. Social justice language teacher education moves beyond critical language teacher education to put the focus squarely on educators' agency and responsibility in effecting both local and broad-scale social change, while seeing their work as embedded in larger societal discourses that shape understandings of 'education' and 'achievement'. Thus, critical educators may work to make explicit understandings of race, class, (dis)ability and so on – markers of difference – and their impact on educational equity and achievement, often resulting in inclusion and representation of these issues in curriculum and materials, and as foci of teacher education. Social justice educators may do this, but also work to understand institutional and societal workings of power, privilege and status (through structures, policies, resource flows and practices), how these affect educational and life opportunities for the students and families they serve, what they are able to do to make their classrooms more equitable and also to effect social/societal change.[1] This work must be done in the classroom, but also renders classroom walls permeable, as students, teachers, administrators, families, community members and organizations collaborate for change. And this is one of the tensions encountered in social justice language teacher education when teachers are focused on their classrooms and schools as they have been prepared to, and must (with ever-increasing 'accountability' measures) do; they may be resistant to taking on broader responsibilities, re-figuring their understandings of their roles and jobs and seeing themselves and their work as 'political'.

Instantiating Social Justice Language Teacher Education

A programmatic initiative

The English as a Second Language (ESL) and Bilingual Education teacher preparation program at my institution is informed, even driven, by just such a social justice perspective. As mentioned earlier, this is a program designed for currently practicing mainstream teachers; it leads to an ESL (and possibly bilingual) teaching credential and, for some, to a master's degree. We attempt to infuse a social justice approach throughout the program, and not limit this to a particular course or set of activities. Thus, a course that teachers take early on introduces them not only to issues in ESL/bilingual education but also to conceptual framings for thinking about the education of English learners. They are introduced to sociocultural theories and critical theories (including those pertaining to communities of practice, power relations etc.) specifically as they relate to schools, families and communities of English learners, and activities are meant to encourage connections between topics and their own practice. This course is intended to provide a 'big picture' framework.

A second course in the program melds second language acquisition theories with teacher research. Teachers conduct a semester-long case study of an English learner, exploring how theories they are reading about play out in the life and body of a particular student. They interview the student, visit the student's home and interact with the student's family, and observe the student in school, thus gaining a first-hand look at language and literacy interactions across the various spaces the student inhabits. This functions, perhaps, as a response to Zeichner's words:

> Although all teacher education programs include at least some direct field experience in schools and sometimes in communities, programs vary as to how much their students are put in contact with students and adults from different backgrounds and the nature of these interactions. For example, some programs emphasize reading and discussing material about issues of race, diversity and equity with very little direct experience with others different than oneself, while others include substantial work in communities where student teachers are positioned as learners rather than as saviors. (Zeichner, this volume: 14)

This experience accomplishes many things, not the least of which is that teachers come to see students as whole beings, not just reduced to the academic competencies and performances that they display in the classroom. They come to recognize the rich resources that children and families possess, what students bring to school and how what students bring is and is not valued, recognized and built on in curriculum, classrooms and school environments. It also positions teachers as learners and students and families as experts, with teachers needing to learn what families have to offer. While this is certainly a component of social justice teacher education (and also a hallmark of culturally and linguistically responsive teaching), it does not, in and of itself, promote social justice.

The analytic focus of this chapter is the second-to-last semester of the program. It is an ESL methods course with a practicum/fieldwork component, and students must have finished all other required coursework (including the two courses mentioned above) prior to taking it.

ESL methods

The Methods course has both a class and a practicum/fieldwork component. Teachers attend class weekly, with each week focusing on a different topic. They fulfill the fieldwork component in their own classrooms; the goal is to tie coursework directly to teachers' practice. Although teachers in the class typically range from teaching at the Kindergarten through high-school levels, in the semester that is the focus here there were eight elementary teachers in the class, and all were women.

Historically, the course has been structured such that students are introduced to 'methods' first, to address issues such as: What is culturally and linguistically responsive pedagogy? How do you incorporate a focus on language into content teaching? What are the language demands of texts, tasks and activities? How do you set both content and language goals for a lesson? How do/should you pay attention to participation patterns in your classroom? Only after attending to these issues, and those of assessment, did we introduce 'Critical Theory/Problem Posing', in week 10 of a 14-week course. And only after Critical Theory did we focus on families (having students conduct home visits), and then, ultimately, address the use of technology in teaching. The message, clearly, was that 'good' teaching and teaching methods came first, and once that was covered, then perhaps we could add on the critical piece, and take into account students' homes and families. Critical approaches and social justice work were add-ons, not central to the curriculum and the work teachers do; they were treated as a separate domain from culturally and linguistically responsive practice, and treated as a 1-week topic.

For this focal semester I rearranged the course. The first class was an introduction to the course, but in the second class (still titled 'Culturally and Linguistically Responsive Classrooms' on the syllabus) we delved into social justice issues and approaches. Teachers read Freire (1985) for his views of social justice education, and Goldstein (2001) for a look at a social justice project with students. We walked through a problem-posing exercise, and explored why such an approach is necessary and right for educating English learners. We overtly discussed institutional, societal and political influences on the education of English learners, acknowledging and exploring reasons for the 'unequal playing field'. Teachers discussed their practices in the light of functioning as agents of change. I then attempted to integrate social justice into every other topic throughout the semester, ensuring that it was central in our discussions and activities. As you will see, this was not always successful. I also replaced a topic from the old syllabus with 'School Climate', to ensure that this important aspect of students' school lives was neither invisible nor ignored by teachers.

In addition to weekly readings and class discussions, students were responsible for conducting and analyzing a home visit (which differed in focus from the one they conducted in the earlier course); having two 'supervisory' visits during the semester, for which they produced lesson plans that were to include, among other things, language goals and a social justice focus, and which they then reflected upon with support from their supervisor; and a culminating 'digital story' of their learning throughout the semester, offering an opportunity for meta-reflection.

As the course designer/instructor, I wanted to track how notions of social justice got taken up and applied throughout the course. To this end, I had the teachers, in the first week of the course, do a quickwrite in response to the question: what is a social justice approach to teaching English learners? I took field notes of class conversations where social justice overtly arose as a topic of discussion, analyzed their lesson plans (produced for the observations) and their digital stories for mention and/or instantiation of social justice issues and approaches, and had them do a second quickwrite during the last class of the semester responding to the same question ('what is a social justice approach to teaching English learners?'). After taking this course, teachers have one more semester that is technically their ESL student teaching, but for which, in practice, I have them work in teacher inquiry groups. They fill out evaluations at the end of the year that encompass both the Methods and the student teaching semesters, and I will use these as evidence as well.

Understanding social justice

The semester began with a quickwrite, enabling me to evaluate perceptions of social justice education that teachers brought to class. Excerpts from their writing include the following:

- Social justice is a word that many people use and that I believe many people have different meanings for. To me teaching for social justice means that each of my students receives a meaningful education.
- Social justice education for ELL students means having the same value put on the ELLs' language/culture/ideas/customs as is put on the students that speak English as a native language. It is a non-judgmental, celebratory, inclusive type of education.

- Students would need to learn in an environment where their culture is accepted & celebrated and learn curriculum that is not geared toward the white privileged students.
- Social justice education for ESL students means they receive services or language support to access the curriculum. Their home languages and cultures are acknowledged, honored, and represented in the schools.
- Social justice ... (for) English language learners means that ELLs are receiving the extra services they deserve to be successful learners and community members. ... Social justice means that all staff in schools are aware that all students, and not just ESL students, are different and have various needs and that they need to teach to those needs.

An analysis of these passages (and others that these are representative of) shows that teachers in this class are aware that schools place differential values on different languages and cultures, and serve some groups of students better than others, particularly along lines of cultural and language difference. There is a focus on valuing what students bring, support services and differentiation in instruction. These are important issues and are, in fact, aligned with at least some of the tenets of linguistically and responsive pedagogy identified above. But, while this clearly reflects awareness of multicultural education, this does not directly address social justice as we have discussed it here. Teachers believed, in fact, what the first teacher quoted above articulated: that social justice really means ensuring access to the curriculum for all students in their class. In my field notes a few weeks later, I say, 'In a follow up to "is ESL just good teaching?" we'll have to discuss "is social justice just good teaching?"' (9/26).

Teachers were focused, as might be expected, on the daily work of teaching in their classrooms and schools, and responded with greater enthusiasm to topics and issues that they perceived could lead directly to ideas for implementation and improvement in practice in ways recognizable to them and to the institutions in which they worked, and to which they were accountable. They acknowledged issues of equity, power relations and so on but were more excited when, for example, the WIDA professional development staff came to present the ACCESS test and WIDA performance indicators[2] in week 4. I began that class by showing a video of five English learners being endlessly tested throughout a day of school, with negative impact on both instruction and learner achievement, and raised a connection between assessment and social justice through a discussion of the current climate of assessment and accountability (especially related to the No Child Left Behind Act) and its impact on English learners in schools. However, although the teachers agreed and vociferously eschewed all the testing that they were required to do, they had keen interest in understanding the significance of the English levels assigned to learners by the ACCESS test, and in learning to use the 'can do' indicators WIDA provides. Although I searched for it in subsequent conversations and work, I could identify no uptake nor ideas generated from teachers that might acknowledge an advocacy role in changing or modifying assessments or standards, making them more equitable, nor in working to mediate the harm that they believed the tests and standards inflict on their students and teaching practice. They appeared, in fact, to be uncritical consumers. I did, throughout the semester, see a lot of uptake and application of the level and performance indicator information WIDA provided.

In approximately the fifth or sixth week of class, teachers were asked to prepare drafts of lesson plans that would serve as the basis of their supervisory observations. At that time teachers were grappling with setting language goals for lessons, which is always one of the primary and most difficult foci of the Methods class. As credentialed and practicing teachers, they had little trouble setting themes and content goals, and designing activities. But when asked to set language goals, and to demonstrate where scaffolding was specifically for English learners in their lessons, and what appropriate assessment for English learners might look like, they struggled. The lesson plans they submitted displayed what I term a 'technicist' approach, that is, a focus on the mechanics of the lesson. So, for example, a math lesson presented looked like this:

Materials Needed:
- Butcher paper
- Sharpie
- Shapes
- Baggies
- Pencil
- Drawing Paper

Lesson Objectives:
- To enhance student thinking and reasoning power about various shapes.
- To develop student interest in learning math.
- To help students explore similarities and differences in shapes.

Language Goals:
- Students will use imperatives by giving directions
- Students will use sequential language (first, then, next, etc.)
- Students will comprehend and use math vocabulary words (line, sides, curve, vertex, vertices)
- Students will ask and answer questions

Prep:
- Make copies of shapes and cut them out
- Put shapes in baggies
- Get paper to draw shapes on
- Get pencils to draw shapes

This was followed by a step-by-step description of the activity, in which the teacher presented the activity, students were placed in groups to do the activity and then students came back together to report out on the activity. As was the case with all of the lesson plans, there was no overt mention of social justice, nor was there any indication that thinking about social justice had been part of the planning. While there was attention across plans to participation patterns – that is, all plans included opportunities for students to work together to make meaning – there was no differentiation, no inclusion of students' funds of knowledge and no connection to home and families, all of which students had mentioned in their initial quickwrites. And there was no connection between the worlds inside and out of school, including, strikingly, a lesson one teacher presented on the civil rights movement in the United States, in which students looked at pictures from the time of and related to the civil rights movement in the 1950s and 1960s, sorted them using a graphic organizer and wrote descriptive paragraphs, but did not engage in any sort of social analysis, discuss the impact on the lives of people involved or consider current parallels.

By early November, the teachers were frustrated. They had been in class for several months, and had gone through their first observation cycle, but felt that they still were not 'getting it'. And they were now in the midst of preparing their second lesson plan. They wanted examples of 'good' lessons, and models of effective practice, especially in terms of setting language goals and infusing language support into content area teaching. A lengthy excerpt from my field notes attests to this.

> Have been slogging along throughout the semester, lots to say about social justice – particularly their understandings – so educating ELs so that they can have better lives (thus doing good teaching for them)

isn't in and of itself social justice. This came out in their lesson plans for the last observation, and it's clearly difficult to learn to set and implement language goals, meet standards, assess, etc., and still have a social justice focus. For this lesson, though, they were reminded to include it, and while the lesson plans tended to move away from math and towards 'critical' topics, there was no overt social justice agenda. A number of them had students contributing information about their families or cultures, and thought this was social justice. So here's what happened in class:

I wanted to pull together all of the loose ends from the semester. The two loosest, to me, are their ability now to identify language functions, but not to identify the specific language for those functions within specific lessons, nor even if they do identify language knowing how to support their students to acquire it. And the second, of course, is their limited understanding of social justice education. So I told them we would be pulling things together, and that one thing I thought still needed work was language goals, and explained the above. They agreed, heads nodding vigorously. I then asked them to go around and say if there was anything they were still struggling with, where they wanted more support. Karen said she thought she had all the pieces from the lessons during the semester, but couldn't pull them together holistically. The others pretty much agreed that they struggle with making lessons 'authentic' – that if they identify language students might need to participate in a lesson, how can they give it to them authentically? And especially given that learners have different English proficiency levels, how to differentiate, and still have it be authentic? We agreed that targeting specific language and forms of language leads to prescription, so how to balance that?

... So then I got to social justice. I asked them to relate the video (of a student engaged in a particular lesson on sending postcards that they had watched) to social justice. They suggested that if the teacher had students talk about where they came from, who was there that they were still in touch with, and how they communicated with them, that would be social justice. I paraphrased, asked if they were saying that if they tied instruction to kids' lives, and let them represent their cultures and backgrounds, then that's educating for social justice? They felt it was. So I said 'I agree that's good multicultural education. But what's the difference between good multicultural education and social justice?' They said that social justice meant that you give the students tools to change their lives. But doesn't that mean that good teaching is social justice? ... They said that social justice education meant making students aware of the larger structures and issues, and how they affected them. Then Karen said that she really struggled with that because, while she understood it, she didn't see what she could do with really young children – how do you bring these issues into instruction with Kindergartners? They wouldn't be able to talk about these things. So we talked about a local teacher's work, which about 3 of them were familiar with. They described him talking with his 1st and 2nd graders about feeling safe, and things that made them feel safe and unsafe. And having them take pictures of their apartments after the fire there, focusing on things that made them feel unsafe. And how he used that as the basis for literacy lessons and effecting social change by writing to the paper and legislators. And planning a march with his students, and getting busted for it by school administrators.

I told them that I really wanted this current lesson plan to reflect social justice, and picked on Hannah – I reminded them of her previous lesson plan on civil rights, and how she had them focusing on issues of race and oppression, and asked what would have made that a good social justice lesson? They said that they'd have to be explicitly aware of the issues, directly talk about them, and connect it to themselves and their lives. I reminded them of problem posing, and we talked about how you could use a problem posing exercise to do that. We talked about having kids explicitly discuss issues of equity and justice, and that it was risky. Somebody said that she'd done something in her class on racism, and there was a middle-class white father in the room helping out, and she was worried, but he loved it. And I pointed out that this isn't only for marginalized kids, but for all kids – that it would be powerful for the white privileged kids to think about this too, and they talked about work out there on white privilege. It was a wonderful discussion.

This discussion seemed to create a tidal shift; social justice issues seemed to become more integral to teachers' thinking and planning afterwards. As noted, lesson plans shifted to include social issues. As an example, one teacher's goals were as follows:

> Students will play with their puppets together and hopefully begin to talk and share in an authentic way for them, while still having the opportunity to view different families interacting in fun ways. This is a good way for young students to make connections and observations about how families in a community might come together, as well as play with families that realistically might not just see each

other outside of school, since some live on the West side of town, and some on the South side.

Here she embeds in the activity of her class – a class with students who represent different race, class and language backgrounds, and live in different parts of town representative of class differences – an opportunity to directly address out-of-school differences and similarities, and to discuss and explore meanings of community across difference. Other teachers had students interview their parents about family traditions, and had students design a storycloth to tie the history of the Vietnamese war to local Vietnamese students and families.

Zeichner, in the introductory chapter, claims, '... there has also been a tension between the academic discourse about teaching for social change and the connection of this discourse to the communities where the work is to be carried out.' While he was addressing the proclivity of teacher education programs and classrooms to read and talk, in lieu of genuine involvement, this is true as well for teachers and students in K–12 classrooms. The teachers, in these lesson plans, made great strides toward breaking down, or permeating, the walls of the classroom, and designed activities whereby students drew the outside world in, while expanding the reach of the classroom out, thus integrating the worlds inside and outside of school. While this is perhaps not, in and of itself, social justice education, it is a clear move toward designing curriculum and instruction that is inclusive, ties to and represents students' lives and families, addresses issues of race, class, culture, language and socio-economic difference and opens up spaces within which social justice work can be done. It is a start.

While the activities themselves displayed movement, a number of the teachers directly addressed 'Social Justice' as a category header in these lesson plans. Comments under these headings read:

Social Justice

> Students will be working on something that is important to them. They will be able to feel proud of their family and share that with the class. All traditions will be valued and validated in the lesson.

Social Justice Rationale

> Even though this is only a group of four, I thought carefully about how to pair the students for this activity. Anna and Ari both have strong personalities and tend to be very vocal. Anna sometimes has trouble understanding directions or questions that are asked of

her and often talks just to talk. Ari will be a good role model for Anna and will help keep her on track. Dami and Nico are both English language learners (ELLs). Dami has strong oral abilities and while normally quiet, lately she has been very excited about reading group activities. Nico's speaking skills are not as strong, and I think Dami will provide the model and peer assistance that he needs to be successful in this lesson.

In these two examples, teachers, when attempting to articulate social justice, are falling back on their original concepts of valuing and validating cultures, and providing scaffolding for all students to participate in class discussion. In the example below, the teacher uses a traditional school activity as a springboard for discussion that may lead to explicit awareness of the effects of culture on student achievement.

Social Justice

> These storytelling activities will be used as a springboard for students to evaluate their own and others' opinions about writing and reading. In a future activity, students will rate different storytelling methods. These survey results will be used to engage students in a discussion of value given to different cultural traditions and the effects that may have for them as students.

Supporting students to gain a meta-awareness of differential values attached to cultural practices is certain a step toward effecting social change, but only, perhaps, in this last example below (the rationale for the puppet activity described above) can we see an explicit articulation of a social justice focus in a themed unit that embeds students' schooling and school experience within a larger (inequitable) community structure, and allows students to explore this through an overarching plan for integrating it into classroom curriculum.

Social Justice Focus

> We are looking at the families of our students, all students in both my ELL class and the bilingual class. Kindergarteners are 'experts' on their own families and what they like to do, where they shop, who lives next door and so on. We are discussing and sharing our families and how they are all different and unique and then how they all interact and are part of a bigger community – our neighborhood, which we will discuss more as we continue our 'Who We Are and Where We're From' unit. This validates and

celebrates each family and allows all students to share one of their funds of knowledge, the way they see their family. It also gives them the opportunity to share their family and how their family interacts/plays with other students who might not normally see them or meet them outside of school, specifically because of racial and economic divides between west and south side families in our school. We will be bringing in pictures of many well- known places in both areas, libraries, parks, stores, restaurants, apartment buildings, churches, Boys and Girls Club and so on. We will also be creating neighborhood maps and focusing our conversations on the fact that our families are all together a big community that lives in neighborhoods and all go to school together. We have started with the focus on themselves and are moving outward to who and what is around them, how it is unique and how it bonds us together in our 'school community'.

Digital stories

The end-of-semester projects, as mentioned earlier, were digital stories of teachers' learning throughout the semester. In this project, meant to support teachers' meta-analysis of their learning, all summed up their current thinking about teaching ELLs, drawing on texts and activities from the semester, and all attempted to articulate their view of effective teaching. Only a few explicitly mentioned social justice, and they are portrayed in the following excerpts. The first:

> When I think back to my student teaching experience, I remember realizing how powerful it was to collaborate with colleagues. This semester I feel that I truly have the opportunity to do this. This not only strengthens the teaching, but the relationships that I have with the teachers and students. I have taken these opportunities to bring up social justice issues into classrooms and have discussions with some colleagues about the strength and power we give to students when we bring this into our classrooms everyday. For me, social justice is a journey. I feel that it is my job as an educator to advocate for my students, encourage colleagues to join this journey, and most importantly, explicitly teach my students how to advocate for themselves.
>
> I wish I could say that I know exactly how to help students advocate for themselves, when sometimes I don't do the best job of it myself. However, I truly believe that students need to figure out who they are, where they come from and where they want to go before any of this

can happen. They need opportunities and safe spaces to explore these ideas. They need an identity.

While this statement is powerful, and illustrates that the notion of advocacy is important to this teacher (she not only articulates this but also shows that she is enacting it), it is also problematic in that she seems to feel that English learners come to school without an identity, thus harkening back to the deficit perspective presented at the beginning of this chapter. Her words seem to suggest that she is unconsciously taking on a patriarchical attitude, wanting to help students without identities, who don't know who they are, on their voyage of discovery. This perhaps points to a flaw in the program; although we do focus on issues of inequitable power relations, we do not have teachers explore their own privilege (or 'whiteness'), as has been advocated by some scholars. This might help to alleviate unconscious positioning on the part of teachers.

In the other example from the digital stories, the teacher, after taking most of the video to discuss WIDA standards, levels and indicators, says:

> ... we were constantly thinking about social justice, and how to level the playing field for our ELLs. While I think this is something I will continue to work towards throughout my career, after much discussion, I do think that validating home cultures and values and allowing students to share that in class is part of teaching in a socially just way.

This demonstrates, again, that understanding and enacting social justice practices is not easy, intuitive or aligned with current educational discourses. This is the same teacher who, in the quickwrite at the beginning of the semester, wrote, 'In an ideal situation, everything in the school would be telling the students "we value you!"' In the quickwrite, she suggests that the school should label everything in students' first languages, and that students should be educated in their home language. Here, at the end of the semester, she brings the work of valuing and validating home languages into the curricular practices of the classroom. While one could argue that this is not social justice – it is good multicultural teaching – for this teacher it is movement in thinking about her practice.

Final quickwrites and evaluations

On the last day of class teachers did a second round of quickwrites in response to the same prompt: what is social justice education for English learners? Excerpts from responses are as follows:

(1)
- giving every child a quality education;
- knowing every child and including who they are in the curriculum;
- getting students the resources they need.

(2) Social justice education is ensuring all my students receive an education that fits their needs. I now also think that it is helping kids to become aware of what is socially just. Along with that aspect is teaching kids how to go about getting the change that they are wanting.

(3) Social justice in the classroom means providing equal access to not only the curriculum, but to awaken awareness in the students of social justice issues that may impact their lives. It means to provide opportunity to achieve equity in education, to hear and assign importance to all students, and to consider ways of integrating family and community cultures.

(4) Social justice is the constant fight for equaling the playing field for everybody. ... Social justice is equal access to education and health care. Social justice is being able to advocate for yourself and your beliefs.

Interestingly, at the end of the academic year, thus a full semester after teachers produced their digital stories and final quickwrites, they filled out an evaluation for the entire year. Throughout the second semester of the year, after the Methods class, we did not directly address social justice (which students complained about on the evaluations – when asked about weaknesses of the program, there were comments such as 'we didn't get many opportunities (in the second semester) to really delve deeply into social issues, despite their importance'; 'need deeper discussions around social justice' and 'need more reading on social justice with action plan!'). Yet when asked what they learned from the program overall, responses included the following:

- That my passion for social justice is justified!
- That ESL teaching is not necessarily just good teaching.
- That issues around ESL teaching and programming come down to issues of equity and social justice.
- That I must advocate for my ELLs, because no one else is.
- Affirmed my thoughts about social justice and its importance and place in schools.
- What it means to be 'engaged' as a community and ways to develop it.

It is safe to say that, at the end of the year, a discourse of social justice had permeated the teachers' learning and thinking. Social justice was important to them, and they clearly wanted yet more of a focus on it than they had had. It is not clear, however, exactly what meanings teachers ascribed to 'social justice', nor how general statements such as these get translated into practice. From my perspective, while I do believe that we constructed a meta-awareness of social justice, and explored social justice issues, we ended the year in early stages of the quest for social justice education.

Conclusion

This chapter, for me, serves as a tool for reflection. I have used it to organize my thinking and analyze my data from the semester. So what have I learned?

I had hoped, in the Methods course, to provide conceptual tools for thinking about social justice work, have teachers develop a meta-awareness of social justice issues, connect their developing understandings of social justice to their communities, lives, students and work and to come to see themselves as agents of social change. In order to do this, I worked to establish a 'community of learners' in my class through having teachers work together to explore their practices, directly connected class content to the situated practices of the teachers, carefully selected readings and scaffolded conversations to focus on social justice issues. I attempted, which perhaps can be interpreted as modeling what I am advocating, to extend course activities and requirements beyond the (university) classroom walls, and to bring the outside world in. I connected schooling and teaching issues, to the extent that I could, to societal and institutional structures that contribute to educational inequities, and kept these sorts of conversations spotlighted.

As is evident, I met with limited success. The notion of 'social justice education' did come to permeate the discourse the group constructed within the university setting, but it was not clear that the teachers consistently applied it to their practices within their school settings. Where it was visible through the artifacts I had to look at, it consisted primarily of focusing curriculum on issues that relate to students' lives, including families, acknowledging a need to advocate for students and ensuring that students could participate in classroom activities. In several cases, it included a focus outside of the classroom, to have students explore their communities and worlds explicitly in terms of equity in social relations, and raising a meta-awareness in students of social justice issues. None, of these, to use a word from Freire, include a component of 'praxis' – there was no direct action for social change. So here are the thoughts I am left with:

(1) Zeichner (this volume) calls for a 'hybrid culture', attempting to do away with hierarchical power structures that typically suffuse teacher education programs. He argues, in effect, that the work of social change cannot happen through the traditional structures of university teacher education programs, but must happen through a re-visioning of the roles of teachers and community members in collaborative endeavors. It is clear that, albeit with the best of intentions, social justice was *my* agenda, and I took every opportunity to impose it on the teachers. This has been a critique of critical theory as well – can we ethically impose a vision of social change? Can we simultaneously impose a vision on people and empower them? Can we impose empowerment? And do we have the right to? Left to somewhat more equitable structures of teacher inquiry groups in the following semester, social justice issues did not, for all intents and purposes, arise, yet there were complaints about that afterwards. So how do we balance power, inquiry and empowerment while attempting to co-construct agency for change?

(2) One consistent theme for me that has run through all of my work is the relational nature of education, learning and teaching, and research. Working with people effectively happens only through relations of trust and respect, and these take time to develop. University courses occur in one 15-week semester, and much must get accomplished without adequate time to build relationships among members of a classroom community. We believe in, and even preach, the local, situated nature of learning, and the need to value, recruit and respond to what learners know and bring in the service of learning. How, in 15 weeks, can we come to understand who teachers are and what they bring, construct a community of learners with relations of trust and respect and engage in the work of learning new approaches and methods while examining practice? Perhaps, rather than setting a fixed endpoint, we embark on the journey, and consider that it is within the journey itself that discoveries and meanings get made together, and these constitute the learning. Everyone participates, everyone learns, though participation and learning do not look the same for all. Thus, locating the sorts of change that I have identified in this chapter represents not a fixed point on a voyage, but simply the current

location of the travelers. This speaks to the need, as illustrated by Toohey and Waterstone (2011, this volume), to engage in ongoing long-term collaborative inquiry, including the messy work of attending to issues of power and voice within the group.

It is not clear to any of us what social justice education looks like in schools and classrooms, nor can it become so. Teachers, classrooms, students and families are idiosyncratic, not uniform, as are the communities and institutions within which they function, and social justice education must be responsive to local situations and conditions. The same can be said for social justice language teacher education; it cannot be prescriptive. I think that the best we can do is to roll up our sleeves and, in the most ethical ways we can devise, get immersed in the messy work of community building for social change.

Acknowledgments

I offer my deepest gratitude to Kathleen Nicoletti and Anneliese Cannon for their ceaseless support and insights throughout this project. And to the teachers –not only for their engagement with the course and with the program, and their inspirational passion for their work and their students, but also for their willingness to allow me to use their work for research and publication purposes. They are the embodiment of dedication, compassion and courage all.

Notes

1. This may be terminological sleight-of-hand; in many instances, 'critical' has been implemented just as it has been described above, although certainly there are educators who consider themselves 'critical' who undertake what I am describing here as social justice work. Nonetheless, we need a distinctive term for marking the explicit meaning offered here.
2. WIDA (World-Class Instructional Design and Assessment) is an organization representing a consortium of states, and its mission is to enhance and assess instruction for English learners. It produces, among other things, a language test (the ACCESS test) that all ELL students in WIDA states take yearly, and a set of performance indicators meant to supplement district content standards for ELLs. The teachers in this study taught in a WIDA state.

References

Cowan, P. and Chung, C. (2007) Latino Language minority students in Indiana: Conditions & challenges. A special report of the center for evaluation and education policy Indiana University. On WWW at http://www.indiana.edu/~iplacc/docs/Language%20Minority%20Report%20CEEP.pdf. Accessed 15.7.2008.

De Jong, E.J. and Harper, C.A. (2005) Preparing mainstream teachers for English language learners: Is being a good teacher good enough? *Teacher Education Quarterly* 32 (2), 101–124.

Dutro, S. and Moran, C. (2003) Rethinking English language instruction: An architectural approach (draft). In G.G. García (ed.) *English Learners: Reaching the Highest Level of English Literacy* (pp. 227–258). Newark, DE: International Reading Association.

Echevarria, J., Short, D. and Powers, K. (2006) School reform and standards based education: A model for English learners. *The Journal of Educational Research* 99 (4), 195–211.

Freire, P. (1985) Reading the world and reading the word: An interview with Paulo Freire (with David Dillon). *Language Arts* 62 (1), 15–21.

Gibbons, P. (2002) *Scaffolding Language, Scaffolding Learning*. Portsmouth, NH: Heinemann.

Goldstein, T. (2001) Hong Kong, Canada: Playwriting as critical ethnography. *Qualitative Inquiry* 7(3), 279–303.

Gonzalez, N., Moll, L.C. and Amanti, C. (2005) *Funds of Knowledge: Theorizing Practices in Households, Communities, and Classrooms*. Mahwah, NJ: Erlbaum.

Hawkins, M. (2010) Sociocultural approaches to language teaching and learning. In C. Leung and A. Creese (eds) *English as an Additional Language: Approaches to Teaching Linguistic Minority Students*. London: Sage Press.

Hawkins, M. and Norton, B. (2009) Critical language teacher education. In J. Richards and A. Burns (eds) *The Cambridge Guide To Second Language Teacher Education*. Cambridge: Cambridge University Press.

Levinson, B., Bucher, K., Harvey, L., Martinez, R., Perez, B., Russell, S., Harris, B., Lucas, T., Villegas, A.M. and Freedson-Gonzalez, M. (2008) Linguistically responsive teacher education: Preparing classroom teachers to teach English language learners. *Journal of Teacher Education* 59 (4), 361–373.

Richards, H.V., Brown, A.F. and Forde, T.B. (2007) Addressing diversity in schools: Culturally responsive pedagogy. *Teaching Exceptional Children* 39 (3), 64–68.

Schleppegrell, M. (2004) *The Language of Schooling: A Functional Linguistics Perspective*. Mahwah, NJ: Erlbaum.

Valdes, G. (1998) The world outside and inside schools: Language and immigrant children. *Educational Researcher* 27 (6), 4–18.

Valdes, G. (2001) *Learning and Not Learning English: Latino Students in American Schools*. New York: Teachers College Press.

Villegas, A.M. and Lucas, T. (2007) The culturally responsive teacher. *Educational Leadership* 64 (6), 28–33.

WIDA Consortium (2007) *WIDA ELP Standards and Resource Guide*. Madison, WI: WIDA Consortium.

Wong Fillmore, L. and Snow, C.E. (2000) *What Teachers Need to Know About Language*. Special Report. Washington, DC: ERIC Clearinghouse on Languages and Linguistics.

Chapter 7
Creating a School Program to Cater to Learner Diversity: A Dialogue between a School Administrator and an Academic

FRANKY POON and ANGEL LIN

Angel's Introduction: Documenting a Journey through a Dialogue

In this chapter, we depart from the traditional register of an academic essay and present a school administrator's (Franky) pioneering journey to start the first school-based program to cater to students with special education needs (SEN) in the form of a dialogue between Franky and Angel (an academic). The school is located in a working-class residential area in a new town in the New Territories of Hong Kong. Although without ample resources, the school, with the committed and innovative work of the school administrator and teachers, has pioneered a program that addresses the basic human right of SEN students to have an appropriate curriculum tailor-made for their needs. The journey is not an easy one, and as the dialogue unfolds, we see the struggles against societal and institutional constraints to create a learning space in which these students can flourish, instead of being drowned in the rigid mainstream one-size-for-all curriculum. With creative human agency and innovative strategies, we see how Franky navigates and negotiates a new path with his teachers and students in this never-easy journey of working for social justice for all children.

Franky's Introduction: Starting a Resource Class to Cater to Learner Diversity

We started a resource class for Secondary One students with SEN in September 2007 in our school. It was set up in response to our three-year school development plan (2006–2009) in which one of the main goals was to increase our school's capacity on catering to learner diversity. With the increasing percentage of students with SEN studying in mainstream schools in Hong Kong, we believed that we should be well prepared to meet such needs by initiating the SEN program in Secondary One.

We provided resource classes in three subjects: Chinese, English and Mathematics. They were designed and monitored by a core team headed by the Vice Principal and assisted by three junior form panel heads of the respective subjects. The resource class for English, like the other two subjects, was conducted in a way similar to an ordinary split class commonly found in schools in Hong Kong for remedial language teaching. No more than 10 students were selected to join the class based on (1) their pre-S1 attainment test results; (2) school-based diagnostic test results (focus: phonemic awareness and sight vocabulary); (3) a one-week lesson observation; and (4) their previous diagnostic reports provided by educational psychologists.

The final placement would be decided if the consents of the following parties were gained: (1) Identification, Placement and Review Committee (comprising all the core SEN team members, the social worker and educational psychologist); (2) parents; and (3) students. The aim of the resource class is to prepare students for full inclusion when they are promoted to S.2.

The resource classes were funded by the Student Learning Support Grant, which has been provided to schools enrolling students with SEN since 2008. In the resource class, each student will have his or her own individual education plan (IEP) (see Appendix 1). In the plan, students' special needs will be identified and addressed. On the basis of a series of diagnostic tests, teachers will help students to set their learning goals, provide learning support and monitor their progress. Each student will have individualized assessments based on his or her IEP.

The resource class in English poses the biggest problems for us. English language has long been given a lot of emphasis in the local school curriculum. Despite the fact that our school adopts Chinese as the medium of instruction (CMI), students are generally pressured into mastering this foreign language well for future academic and career success. However, as most of our students come from working-class families, their exposure and motivation to learn English is generally low (see Lin, 2005). In our English resource class, we also need to deal with students with learning difficulties. It is not hard to imagine the frustration that students with dyslexia face when they are forced to learn a foreign language. Therefore, through the resource class, we aim to rebuild students' confidence and basic skills in acquiring this socioeconomically important language in Hong Kong.

While lesson materials are tailor-made for students' individual needs, all students will be provided with the following core curriculum that covers the following:

- Phonics
- Reading Comprehension and Strategies
- Vocabulary Development and Part of Speech
- Writing (Text Types and Punctuation)
- Grammar (Tenses and Usage)
- Speaking/Listening
- Language Arts

Franky and Angel's Dialogue

Now we represent the dialogue between Franky and Angel, with Franky reflecting on his journey in the past few years and Angel responding to and eliciting further reflections from Franky. The dialogue has been organized into different themes that were deemed important by Franky in documenting the challenges that he came across in his journey of starting the SEN program. For each theme, we have an introduction by Franky, followed by selected passages from the exchange between Franky and Angel. The passages have not been edited. The dialogue was exchanged over e-mail from March to May in 2010. When the dialogue came to a certain point, Angel wrote a section on summarizing feedback and then invited Franky to write a summary section to reflect on what he thought he might have gained in the process of dialoguing with Angel.

Who should join?

March 29, 2010
Dear Angel,

There are a few issues that we would like to address when we are implementing a pull-out program for Secondary One students who have severe difficulty in learning English.

We call this pull-out program 'resource class' as the teacher–student ratio is less than 1:10. The first question that confronted us was 'who to pull out' from the classroom. Our first idea was that those who were diagnosed with dyslexia, mild-grade intellectual disability and autism would be automatically placed in the resource class for intensive support. As an administrator, it was also a politically correct way to proceed as those students could each receive an extra grant ranging from $10,000 to $20,000 from the government. To employ an extra teacher to teach them in the resource class seemed to be the correct thing to do. However, our classroom observation (which started on the first school day and lasted for a week) revealed that some of those identified as having SEN could learn quite well in a bigger class. Some of them were able to listen to and understand teachers' instruction and complete tasks on their own or in groups. However, a few students who had no SEN diagnosis did not seem to benefit from our teaching in the first week. Some of them also had behavioral problems and refused to participate in class at all.

Facing this dilemma, all S.1 English teachers, the SEN coordinator and me (VP) sat together to discuss the placement of students in the resource class. We came up with a lot of conflicting views, which include the following:

(1) We shouldn't rely too much on the diagnosis reports as our aim of setting up a resource class was to give those who could not learn in the big class intensive support. That hopefully could help them get back to a mainstream classroom in S.2. The needs perceived by teachers were therefore more important than the clinical labels that were assigned to them a year or years ago.
(2) However, some form teachers were worried that parents of students with special needs would complain if they were not given intensive support that they thought they were entitled to.

Finally, we made a compromise between the two: allowing some students who could be supported in a mainstream class to study in a resource class while reserving two places for needy students without SEN reports.

Angel, as a language teacher, what decision should we make and what should it be based on when making such a decision? What role should students' previous clinical diagnosis play in teachers' pedagogical decisions and choices?

Franky

April 3, 2010
Dear Franky,

I think your class observations provide the best guidance. However, other political and administrative issues (e.g. parents' potential misunderstanding) get in the way of exercising your educational judgment. Your solution is a compromise between what's educationally sound to do and what's politically correct to do.

If there can be more trust between parents and the school, would the above problem be solved? If the parents can be involved in the meeting and the discussion determining who should join the pull-out program, will there be more chances of achieving better understanding on the part of the parents? There's no single right way to do things, and I believe you and your colleagues have made the best decision based on your judgment and your constraints. What do you think?

Angel

April 4, 2010
Dear Angel,

You are right! We did find that getting the parents involved in deciding the kind and level of support for their children was useful. By explicitly stating the purpose of resource classes and the selection criteria during our first meeting with S.1 parents in July, we saved a lot of time negotiating with parents the kind of support that they could expect to get from school. We repeatedly emphasized that resource classes were set up to prepare students with severe difficulties for learning in an inclusive classroom in S.2. Gaining parents' trust in teachers' decisions on student placement is extremely important.

Franky

April 9, 2010
Dear Franky,

That sounds great! In your working together with parents, have there been any memorable events or significant incidents that you remember you can share with others (other teachers and schools)?

Angel

April 10, 2010
Dear Angel,

One of the most extreme cases that we have this year is about a S.1 student who has spent 6 years studying in a special school before coming to our school. He has mild grade intellectual disability. However, his verbal communication is comparatively strong. We admitted him because (1) his brother is our current student; (2) the underachievement of the student is partly due to his unsupportive parents; (3) we see lots of potential in the student despite his poor family support; (4) we are touched by the support and dedication of his old-aged grandpa who provides all the love and care for the two brothers.

The problem is that the student seemed to have learned nothing 'academic' in his previous study. His lack of basic literacy and numeracy skills make it nearly impossible for him to benefit from the mainstream curriculum. To help him to start from scratch, we placed him in resources classes for Chinese, English and Mathematics. We provided him with one-to-one tutorial sessions to learn to write and read. We appointed him to be the class monitor so that his good verbal skills can be put to use. We provided him with modified examination papers to assess his learning progress. After half a year, his progress was impressive. He even asked teachers to allow him to take the mainstream examination papers.

However, starting from March this year, he began to show symptoms of epilepsy. Occasionally, he would suffer from seizures that would paralyze him for a few minutes. His parents thought it could be caused by the pressure from his study and requested that he be placed back to the special school. What impresses us most is that the student refused, saying that he enjoyed his study and life here at our school. He promised he would try to take good care of himself so that he could continue to study here. Sure, we also let all teachers know his medical conditions and suggest measures to help him. Angel, I don't know if that is a relevant case to illustrate how we communicate with parents, students and teachers in order to maximize our support to each student.

Franky

April 16, 2010
Dear Franky,

This case is touching and you and your colleagues have worked magic for this student. Sometimes parents are the sources of problems and they are tough cases to crack especially when they refuse to recognize that they might be one of the sources of the child's difficulties. What you and your school did for the student is precisely what it means to empower a student: you empower him with the ability to see his own strengths and his own power and capacity to learn: now that he knows what he can achieve under the right conditions, and he knows his own strengths (his strong verbal skills he uses when he performs his duties as monitor), and he even asks to take the mainstream exam papers: see how much self-confidence he's gained within a short time if given the right soil and right care, just like a plant with great growing capacity if it's given the appropriate nutrients to grow (e.g. water and sunshine)! Under these circumstances: empowering the student him/herself so that they can stand up for their own rights and speak for their own benefits ('cause they know which school they enjoy and which school/program allows them to grow and shine) against their parents who, alas, oftentimes remain a main source of the problems! When the child has been empowered, it's not just us (the school or the teachers) who are advocating for his rights and benefits, but he himself can advocate for his own benefits ☺! That's the best kind of help one can give to another: not just material help, but also empowerment: helping another person to be able to help himself/herself!

Angel

Who to teach?

March 29, 2010
Dear Angel,

Another controversial issue that took up quite a lot of our discussion time was 'who to teach them?' If the resource class is an extra pull-out program funded by the Student Learning Grant for SEN students, students should be taught by contract teachers funded by the Grant. However, we had a quite heated debate over it as some teachers argued that contract teachers were often inexperienced. So our question is:

Should we deploy an experienced teacher to teach the resource class?

If yes, is it unfair to the mainstream students who may be taught by inexperienced teachers? What would happen if the higher achievers were adversely affected by such an arrangement? Are we depriving their rights to be taught well?

Franky

April 3, 2010
Dear Franky,

Yes, this is indeed a tricky question! How did you overcome it? What teachers did you deploy in the end? I guess one can try out a team-teaching method; i.e. experienced teachers will be team teaching with the contract ones, and gradually letting the contract teachers take over the teaching duties of the pull-out class? Again there's no perfect solution, but one just needs to think of creative ways of getting out of these administrative dilemmas? Let me know your views.

Angel

April 4, 2010
Dear Angel,

We decided to deploy the most experienced teachers to teach the resource classes. We believe that only experienced teachers have a more comprehensive understanding of the curriculum and, therefore, they can be more able to flexibly design and deliver the curriculum based on students' individual needs. We also invited two experienced teachers to become the mentors of the less experienced ones. Because of the constraints of manpower, we did not manage to try out a team-teaching method. We tried to compensate it with regular peer observations between the experienced and less experienced teachers.

Franky

April 9, 2010
Dear Franky,

That sounds very sensible! How long do you think it will take before the less experienced teachers can be mentored to be able to teach these classes on their own? What are the factors in making this expert–novice peer observations and mentoring successful? What do you think makes this work better in your schools than other situations (if you think this mentoring model and practice do work successfully in your school)? What do you think other schools (in a similar situation as yours) can learn from your experience in this area? What advice can you give to other school practitioners and administrators?

Angel

April 10, 2010
Dear Angel,

Those are very good and important questions. The first magic word is 'system'. To make it work in any school, there should be a clear mentoring system to support this kind of 'expert–novice' professional relationship, which is not something optional for the less experienced teacher to enter into. We've made it very clear to the new teachers that their assigned mentors are colleagues that they need to work closely with. We've built collaborative lesson planning and peer observations into the timetable, though the actual frequency may be decided by teachers. We also have communicated our expectations to the mentors, specifying their roles in the mentees' professional development and holding them accountable for their mentees' performance. The mentors are also involved in the appraisal of the new teachers, which significantly empowers them as mentors.

Another magic word is 'trust'. A system is only an empty shell if there is no trust in it. Through our internal staff sharing and development activities, we reiterate the importance of trust between colleagues. The building of trust among colleagues ultimately benefits our students as trust allows us to be more honest and open to discover problems (either from the teachers, school policy and administration) and work out collaboratively the solutions to them. Trust is more about values and attitude and it has to be fostered in a supportive school culture. Angel, I don't know if that is too abstract for other schools to make reference to.

Franky

April 16, 2010
Dear Franky,

System and trust: that's very good organizing words to summarize the systematic policies and structures that you have established in your school to enable such kind of expert–novice mentoring to succeed. Good systems or structures will be a long-term guarantee of good practices, and other schools can certainly learn from the conducive structures and the productive practices that you established in your school. I guess that's how we share our experience with others: not just by describing the details, but also by summarizing the key factors, or key structures and practices which seem to work in one place, and it's up to others to explore whether they can adapt your structures and practices in their own contexts which might share similarities (albeit also with differences). That's also what we, academics or theorists, do: to summarize the key factors and structures and practices, so that these good 'things' can be sharable and discussable: i.e. they can be critically reflected on, discussed, analyzed, and thus they can be adapted and tried out in other contexts. What do you think? Do you think you can also do this job of summarizing and 'theorizing' apart from your great role of practitioner and pioneer? As you're doing a lot of sharing work with other teachers and schools these days, do you feel that you're actually summarizing and theorizing your own practices so that you can share them with others in a systematic way? What kind of theoretical resources (or tools) do you think you can acquire to help you do this job even better?

Angel

What to teach?

March 29, 2010
Dear Angel,

Instead of adapting the textbook to cater to students' needs in the resource class, we designed our own curriculum and materials for the English class focusing on phonics, sight words (high-frequency words), reading aloud and comprehension strategies. Through routine activities that aimed to develop their phonemic awareness, we found that students had marked improvement in their decoding skills and their motivation. All of them were willing to sound out unknown or unfamiliar words and were willing to communicate with teachers in English. They were also encouraged to do lots of self-access learning by using information technology software and completing graded worksheets in their folders. Instruction was cut to the minimal, so that the teacher could provide more individual support to each student.

However, some parents felt very uneasy about the absence of a textbook. Some complained that the learning of phonics was childish and could not help prepare their children for the requirement of public examinations. Some said that teachers should try to boost students' standard so that they could complete the tasks in the textbook. To throw away the textbook means teachers, parents and even students themselves had no idea about their standard. So, how should we treat the textbooks and how should they be related to students' learning? If students are engaged in communicative tasks in class and are willing to take initiative in their learning, are we preparing them for their learning in upper forms? How should a curriculum in one form be linked to another form? What should they learn before they can benefit in an inclusive classroom in S.2?

How to assess?

Assessment is also an issue puzzling us a great deal. As each student in the resource class has an IEP and what they learn depends on where they are, how should a summative assessment paper be set? Should we set eight different papers for eight different students? How individualized should the assessment be and how could we judge if a student has done his or her best when there is no comparison with others?

We ended up setting two different papers: one for the students with specific learning difficulties (dyslexia, autism and ADHD) and one for the mentally disabled and slow learners. For the latter group, more visual cues were used to help them to comprehend the texts or instructions.

As for the report card, we put an asterisk next to their subject marks to indicate that they have attempted a modified assessment paper.

Franky

April 3, 2010
Dear Franky,

These are indeed very important questions. Let's use a metaphor: a patient has been relying on a pair of glasses to correct their eyesight; however, we know that the pair of glasses is not really helpful, but psychologically it gives the person and his parents some reassurance about it, as everybody else is wearing this kind of glasses. One day, a really knowledgeable doctor comes along and suggests taking away the glasses and training the person to do corrective surgery plus postsurgery viewing exercises to train the patient in correct viewing postures. The patient and his parents are very nervous and uncomfortable about trying these new ways.

So, yes, we need to design new ways of assessment so as to re-establish the confidence of the public about your new ways of teaching and developing curriculum materials which are beyond the confining boxes of textbooks. It will take some time, and some rigorous assessment and curriculum development research to prove to the public (parents, students, funding bodies, school principals, etc.) that the new teaching methods and curriculum materials will achieve those learning objectives specified/required by public exams. Does this make sense to you at all? We can have both the new curriculum and new pedagogy, plus some exam skills workshops to supplement the new curriculum; i.e. it's not an either–or situation? Do you think this might be feasible?

Angel

April 4, 2010
Dear Angel,

 I totally agree with you. In fact, the new senior secondary school curriculum and its forthcoming public examinations allow a more flexible curriculum to be delivered at school. In the previous/existing public examinations, the performance of students is based on norm-referencing. The grades that students get do not tell us anything about what they are able to do in a particular subject. In fact, we are just comparing the performance of one student against that of their counterparts from the same cohort. As a result, we can only teach everything from the syllabus, hoping that our students would be able to perform better than the others. However, the new public examination is based on standards-referencing. For each level (grade), a clear set of descriptors is provided to illustrate what students should be able to do in order to reach a particular level. Here, differentiation of the CONTENT for individual students is possible. For those who experience severe learning difficulties in a particular subject, more realistic learning targets can be set and made known to students. Instead of covering the whole examination syllabus, teachers can help select the kind of content and practices that are pitched at students' level. This gives students a sense of ownership of their learning and they are encouraged to set their own learning targets in each subject. However, to realize it in classroom teaching and learning, more research or experience needs to be gained and shared. Do you think it is feasible?

Franky

April 9, 2010
Dear Franky,

 Yes, I think this is not only feasible but the only way to get these students working toward some realistic goals and not getting frustrated! I think you're doing the right thing for them. Also, setting realistic goals doesn't mean that we're 'dumbing down' the curriculum for these students as long as we have got it clear in our mind and in our planning about what kind of routes these students will take to eventually reach similar targets: they might take a longer route and not the same route as other students, but we must try to map out (together with the students) the routes that will take them 'there' eventually, so as not to limit their eventual success. Do you think this is what you sense to be the case in your situation?

Angel

April 10, 2010
Dear Angel,

Exactly! Through careful differentiation in curriculum, learning materials and tasks, pedagogy and assessment, we are trying to maximize the number of possible choices for our students with very diverse needs. At the same time, we must also clearly articulate to students, parents and the public that these multiple pathways are leading to the same goal: maximizing the potential of each student. Not only can students be allowed to learn in their own way and at their own pace, they can also be made aware of the other choices available in the classroom and the school. None of them would feel uncomfortable being different from others as they all have a respectable goal to pursue.

Franky

April 16, 2010
Dear Franky,

How successful do you think you and your colleagues have been to get this message across to the shareholders (e.g. parents, EDB, School Superviory Board members, etc.)? Any difficulties encountered? What strategies helped you to overcome them? How, in the long run, do you think this message should be promoted in the society at large so that the public (parents, govt. officials, legislative councilors, etc.) will get this important message: respecting diversity, respecting the diverse learning needs and styles of different kinds of students? What needs to be done in the long run, by different parties, and by you, or your school? What role can you and your school play in this mission and vision?

Angel

How should they be taught?

March 29, 2010
Dear Angel,

All resource class lessons were conducted in an activity room equipped with the following facilities:

10 computers (one for each student), an electronic whiteboard, a visualizer, a desktop computer connected to a hi-fi system and a color laser printer, 10 movable tables for flexible grouping and individual work, a board to display students' achievement and a cabinet storing their folders, dictionaries, card games and other learning materials.

The space allows students to do a lot of multisensory activities. We found that most of our resource class students were those who enjoyed more body movement (kinesthetic learners) while they were learning. I guess that was the main reason a crowded traditional classroom could not cater to their needs as they were always the troublemakers. We maximized their opportunities to move around by encouraging them to go to different places to perform different tasks.

We know our students are doing very well in the resource class; however, what should be done to prepare them for their learning in a bigger and a more crowded class where physical movement/response is constrained?

Franky

April 3, 2010
Dear Franky,

Perhaps, there can be a gradual transition period for these students. After they have built their skills and confidence working in a classroom environment, we might gradually decrease the frequency with which they can move around? One way might be to explicitly and directly discuss with these students this dilemma: 'Now we're in a pull-out class, we can move around easily; however, our aim is to get you back to the regular class as that's what all students need to do in the end, because government funding will last only for a year (or a limited period of time); after that we will have to put you back; also, it's good for you to be back to the regular class as that way you can enjoy the status of a regular student. Now, can you help us (the teachers) to think of ways of making this transition easier for you?'

If we're open and sincere and invite students to discuss with us and contribute to the possible solutions, perhaps we can gain their understanding and their active input in solving this problem? If we think that we're not solving all the problems for them, but gradually enabling them/empowering them to gain a grasp of their own situation (including their strengths and weaknesses, and the problems and dilemmas facing them) and invite them and co-construct with them solutions (or partial solutions) to these problems, perhaps we're really helping them to help themselves? However, I don't know if this sounds feasible to you at all?

Angel

April 4, 2010
Dear Angel,

I do agree with you that inviting students to discuss with teachers about the purpose and arrangement of school support (resource class) is the best way to empower students. The concept that we are trying to co-construct with students' solutions to their problems in learning is important. More often than not, students are just passive recipients of our 'assistance'. As a result, they are alienated from their own problems and do not have any motivation to solve them. Teachers may see it as indifference on the part of students and fail to notice that it is actually their fault for not allowing students to actively take part in identifying and suggesting solutions to their own problems. Angel, that is a very important shift of thinking. But how can I help teachers to reflect on this issue?

Franky

April 9, 2010
Dear Franky,

I guess teachers will understand this if they see you working together with them to find their solutions to problems that they have: i.e. you're not 'giving' them your well-thought-out solutions, but you're engaging them to discuss with you and to explore with you together to find solutions to the teaching problems that they face. Then by drawing a parallel between this and their students, they might be able to be led to see that in the same way, they can invite and engage their students to work together with them to find solutions to the students' learning issues ... i.e. like what you said, students are not alienated from their own problems, and likewise, teachers are not alienated from their own problems, and we're all learning together and with each other, then perhaps we can build a community of practice that believes in the practice of 'not giving solutions to others', but working together to find solutions together? What do you think? Do you feel that this might be feasible in your situation?

Angel

April 10, 2010
Dear Angel,

You nailed it. Ownership is what I have been promoting in my school. You don't feel satisfied to own someone's solutions, let alone their problems. A lot of common phrases flying around schools include 'You don't understand my problems/my class', 'Your suggestions can't help solve my problems', 'OK, tell me what to do?' All these show a lack of community of practice and 'collaborative ownership', which may be detrimental to the development of a school.

Franky

April 16, 2010
Dear Franky,

If you're to share this belief and practice with other school principals or administrators, what are your best strategies to do so? What will you present to them to get them to understand this 'idea' or this basic principle of 'ownership', and how can you use your own examples to illustrate this idea? Have you ever done this sharing with other school personnel? What's your experience like? What have you learnt from these experiences?

Angel

Whom should they learn with?

April 29, 2010
Dear Angel,

After a year of implementation, we did find that students in resource class showed marked improvement in terms of phonological awareness and reading fluency. They were also more motivated and engaged. However, one thing that really worried us was the fact that they did need to get back to the big class in S.2. Unless we are able to differentiate the learning materials and employ appropriate instructional methods, the students with special needs may lag behind again and lose their motivation. What should we do to prepare them to learn with other students whose ability and language skills are much stronger than theirs? Is there a threshold level by which we can judge whether a student can benefit from a bigger class?

More fundamentally, should we pull them out in the first place? By pulling them out from their original classroom, do we deprive them of a chance to interact with other students in a mainstream classroom?

Franky

April 3, 2010
Dear Franky,

   This is indeed a dilemma: in the ideal situation, we can have a transition period to help them gradually adapt back to the mainstream class. Let's consider this metaphor: a wild lion was accidentally hurt in the forest and if left in the wild it will certainly not survive. The zoo takes the animal into its foster care and shelters it by providing special medical and nutritional care. After a while, the lion has recovered and now we're faced with the dilemma: should we keep it in the zoo or should we put it in a transition program to gradually help the lion to get back to its wild life: i.e. to find food for itself? Perhaps we can design a transition program to teach the students some strategies to survive in the big class context; we can also continue to have some kind of extra support class (in addition to the mainstream big class) so as to give extra help/instruction to the students to adapt to the mainstream context (if funding allows); there is no single solution, but we can try out different possible solutions, perhaps?

Angel

April 4, 2010
Dear Angel,

   Thanks for the metaphor. I understand that the experience in a zoo for a lion can never substitute that of its wild life. But what if the wild life is so cruel that only the fittest can survive? There is not much that we the zookeepers can do to prepare the most disadvantaged students for a highly selective and exclusive system of our society. Despite the attempt of many of my teachers who tried to provide additional help to students with special education needs in a mainstream classroom, some students still find their learning experience frustrating and express the view that they want to quit their studies once they reach 16. I guess there is something more fundamental concerning the kind of 'wild' life that we want our society to provide to each of its inhabitants.

Franky

April 9, 2010
Dear Franky,

   Yes, you're absolutely right on this. You remind me of the importance of the researcher's role in not only 'describing the world' but also in 'changing the world'. This might need to take the form of some long-term advocacy work: trying to change the government's policy regarding resource allocation, especially to enable students with diverse learning needs and learning styles/routes to be able to do so. It takes more than just research, but also takes a lot of savvy connecting and working to change policy makers' decisions. In your work for the EDB, do you feel that you might stand a chance of getting into touch with some policy makers, and of having a rare chance of influencing them? What do you think it will take to influence EDB/govt. policies? Perhaps the parents' groups can form some pressure groups to give pressure to the govt.? And what will your role be in this, if any? What kind of support might you be able to give to the parents (e.g. the kind of educational principles and rationales so that they can argue and negotiate with the govt.?) So researchers and school administrators can work with parents in the long run to advocate for policy change? Does it all sound too idealistic? Do you see any possibility of achieving this in the long run?

Angel

April 10, 2010
Dear Angel,

These are not at all idealistic! For the past three years, I have been working with EDB on half-time secondment in the project titled: Whole-school approach to catering for learner diversity. I have been given a lot of opportunities to share in many teacher seminars. Many teachers have been inspired by our work and they start to initiate some school-based projects to better cater for the diverse needs of students in their schools. As for our influence at the policy level, I guess we still have a very long way to go. Our government is such a huge bureaucracy to penetrate. Many of the officials that I know are only street-level bureaucrats who have no influence on policy making. Despite the fact that most of them appreciate our work and agree with our mission and ideals, they have no say in the government to effect any significant change.

Parents are our biggest assets. This year, I started to go out more often to give parent talks in community centers. My sharing is often greeted with heavy nodding and tears from parents. Many of them are too helpless to even be aware of the basic rights of their kids. Their children's inability to fit into our rigid education system and practice is often depicted as their own deficiency as parents. They have no one to blame but themselves. I believe that the increasing participation of parents in advocating their children's right to equity and quality education is an irreversible trend.

I also think researchers have a very important role in making such change. They are the ones who could provide well-supported evidence of the deficiency of our existing system. They can also draw upon worldwide research and literature and provide the policy makers and, most importantly, the public viable choices for public dialogues to take place. Don't forget that our society, like many others, has a very high regard for academics. Angel, do you think that is something that research can and should do?

Franky

April 16, 2010
Dear Franky,

Yes, I do think this is what research can and should do, and that's why I think our dialogues are useful as we bring different resources (my theoretical resources and your frontline experiences) to bear on the issues. I just would like to challenge you to think in a bit more political terms: if one day some parents want you to speak as an expert witness for them to negotiate with the govt. on some policy issues regarding provision of educational services for their children, how would you respond to that, and what kind of systematic, professional evidence can you give to help them?

Angel

Resource class: Deficiency versus development

March 29, 2010
Dear Angel,

We spent a lot of time identifying gaps in students' learning. Our approach – diagnostic-prescriptive teaching – does help us to identify areas for intervention. However, the focus on deficiency may prevent us from seeing and teaching to the strengths of students. Instead of relying on a deficiency model, is there a more development-oriented model on which we design our curriculum, pedagogy and assessment?

Franky

April 3, 2010
Dear Franky,

This is a very good question; yes, we must leave the deficiency model, and instead adopt a 'difference model'; i.e. they are not deficient but they have different learning styles and require different teaching methods. The 'gaps' are not 'deficiencies' but 'differences'; these students might have strengths that do not count as strengths in the mainstream learning game. You're definitely right about this.

Angel

April 4, 2010
Dear Angel,

It is really hard for us as frontline teachers to negotiate space for our students in a system in which talent is narrowly defined and expressed. I believe that it is our society which fails to recognize, develop and celebrate many talents from our diverse student population. Your suggestion of a 'difference' model may pave the way for a more inclusive education system which values diversity and its contribution to both classroom teaching and learning. It also helps us to reflect on what should be considered when we are talking about student achievement. Attached with this file please find two pieces of student works from a Form Two student who has mild-grade intellectual disability and autism (see Appendix 2). This student is actually a rare case in mainstream secondary schools in Hong Kong as students with multiple exceptionalities are usually placed in special schools. You can see from his works he is very talented!

Franky

April 9, 2010

Yes, Franky, I think you're right, and it takes a long time to change the public's (the general public, including policy makers) views and to change their prejudices so that they will start to respect students with diverse needs and diverse learning routes. But it will never happen (i.e. social change, and people's attitude change) if we do not start doing something, no matter how small-scale it is ... Just as the works that you show me, if more people (the general public, the society at large, the govt. officials, the politicians, etc.) can be exposed to more of these talented works of our students with diverse needs, perhaps their minds can change about them, and the policies can change about them? Remember just 100 years ago, no women could ever go to school but see what social change has happened today. But of course, we hope that it won't take 100 years for us (or our next generations) to see change in the society's thinking and in our education system ... what do you think? What can we do to facilitate this social and educational change, no matter how small our impact in the short run will be? This is also what's meant by working for social justice, and it seems that we can all be doing this, although only in very small ways perhaps, but nonetheless important ways ...

Angel

April 10, 2010
Dear Angel,

You can never achieve anything big if you don't do small things right. I guess we can start by gathering, organizing and presenting small successful cases to the public. We have to redefine the narrowly defined 'success' in our society by presenting alternative cases. Only by competently showing real cases can we persuade others to believe the otherwise. Discussion that often stays on the theoretical and philosophical level can never effectively change our practice and the existing system. I often tell stories in my presentations to teachers, parents and government officials. My experience tells me that real stories are powerful in changing people's deep-seated biases. What do you think? Do you think as a researcher, you can contribute to this storytelling thing at another level?

Franky

April 16, 2010
Dear Franky,

You're right about the need for real-life examples and stories.

The govt. believes in statistics and data, while the public can be persuaded by real-life cases. Thus, I think we need to do both and use a range of different strategies to gather evidence and to present them in multiple ways/formats, both with real-life examples/stories and with solid research test data to show the students' improvement in their skills and knowledge if provided with the kind of instruction appropriate to their diverse learning needs and styles. We need to adopt a wide range of methods and formats to gather and present the evidence, and to give them the kind of professional, legitimate status, just like medical research data does, so that advocacy work can be done on multiple fronts; pure theory, or pure stories alone are much less effective than if we can combine both of them, and for different audiences using different proportions of them ☺? What do you think?

Angel

Angel's summary section

April 29, 2010
Dear Franky,

Reading your reflection on the dilemma and questions that you and your colleagues encountered reminds me of the always 'situated' nature of educational practices: i.e. the principles we learn and teach are abstract, but the problems and students and parents we face are always situated in concrete contexts, which are much more complex than the textbook cases of teaching principles. However, I hope this does not make you feel pessimistic, because just as the problems are situated, the potential methods of tackling the problems (i.e. solutions) are also situated: i.e. they are in the situation for you to discover. That means no general principles/educational concepts alone can help us anticipate and find solutions to our situated problems and dilemmas. However, when we're situated in our contexts, we'll develop situated competencies to extend and apply these educational principles in a situated way that is appropriate to our context. In this situation, you just need to believe in your intuition (which is actually based on your observations of all the complex features of your situation) and your creative adaptation of the principles to find ways to tackle the dilemmas. And interacting with both academic researchers and other experienced colleagues who have gone through similar situations (which, however, in your case, might include mainly you yourself ☺!) might help. Does the above make sense?

Please write your responses and feelings and views to the above. Feel free to say: no, what you said is too idealistic! Or, no, I don't think what you said make sense in my situation, because ... I look forward to reading your responses and views!

Angel

May 1, 2010
Dear Angel,

Your suggestion of the situated nature of educational practices really strikes a chord with me. My teachers and I always look for practical solutions to problems confronting us outside our contexts. However, we often feel frustrated as no matter how clearly articulated the practices are, when it comes to transferring them to our own setting, we are faced with so many problems during implementation. Your idea of creatively adapting the principles we learn from research or previous experience is both inspiring and encouraging. We should believe in our judgment and even intuition when solving problems which are deeply embedded in our unique context. Only by appreciating the complexities of contexts can we be able to come up with the most practical and relevant solutions.

Franky

May 8, 2010
Dear Franky,

Yes, I think we can strike a balance between reading from the books, learning from other experienced educators and exploring solutions in our own situated practice. I guess if we keep our minds open, the multiple ways of getting help and getting insights are helpful ... the education theories, the practitioners, and our own situated observations and explorations – they all offer different perspectives to look at our issues and problems ... I guess the ability to look at things from different perspectives, and to gain insights from different perspectives will also do us good; what do you think? Truth does not reside in the theorist, nor in the practitioner, but seems to be in the creative and innovative interactions and inter-illuminations of them, when we can succeed in bringing together different perspectives, and different kinds of expertise to bear on our problems?

Angel

May 9, 2010
Dear Angel,

Totally agreed. In fact, many of our current problems come from our inability to bring in different perspectives and viable alternatives. Our rigidity in defining problems, identifying solutions and executing measures sometimes does more harm than good. Do you think that is a fair comment?

Franky

May 10, 2010
Dear Franky,
   Definitely ☺!

Angel

Franky's summary section

May 15, 2010
Dear Angel,

   To make our voice heard and message understood has long been a pressing issue for teachers in my school. I honestly know our school is doing the right things for our students. Instead of lacking a tool to help our students, we are lacking a tool to explain to others (the government, the public, parents and teachers) why our students need to be helped the way they are. We are not short of strategies to deal with the problems of our students but we are seriously short of the right words to convince others.

   Angel, the conversation that has been taking place between us has forced me to face this issue head-on. Perhaps even without your knowing, you have provided me with the necessary theoretical resources which help me to conceptualize my thinking and practice. The terms that you occasionally use, such as advocacy, help put my work into perspective and link it to a wider community of research and practice.

   If you look at the words or phrases that you used in your previous responses, you can discover the following concepts: 'theorizing', 'summarizing', 'systematic', 'professional evidence', 'sharing', 'getting the message across' and 'promote' etc. Through our dialogues, I am given the opportunities to reflect on, to conceptualize and reconceptualize my everyday practices and encounters.

   Your questions also force me to reconsider my role as an educator in relation to other parties: the government, parents, other teachers and the public. I am honestly not sure how I could influence others but I guess I myself should be the first one to be inspired by my own work before anyone else could be inspired.

   Below are some of the slides taken from presentations I have given, see if they can serve the purpose of theorizing and summarizing.

3-tier intervention model for catering to learner diversity

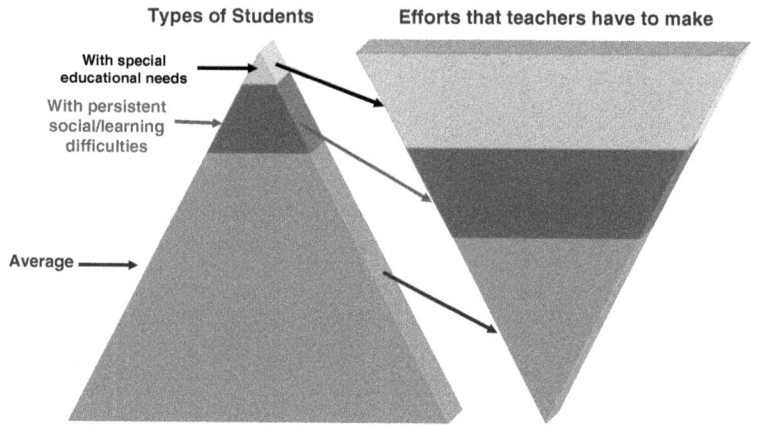

Catering for diversity is a shift from selection to inclusion

Creating a School Program to Cater to Learner Diversity

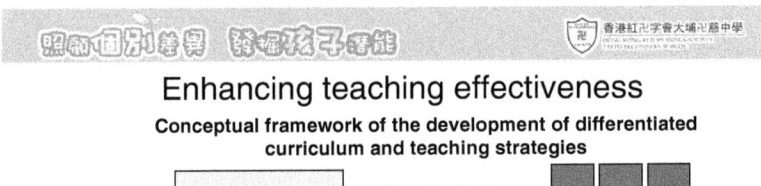

Enhancing teaching effectiveness
Conceptual framework of the development of differentiated curriculum and teaching strategies

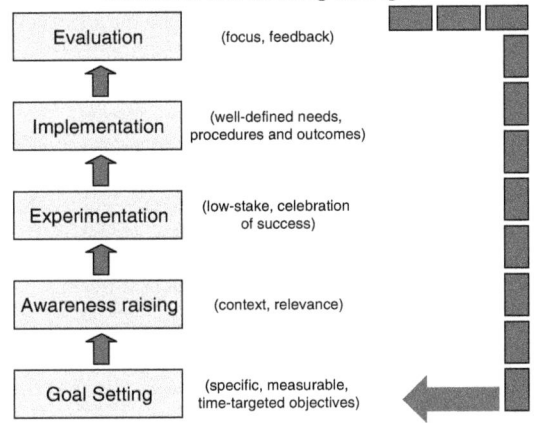

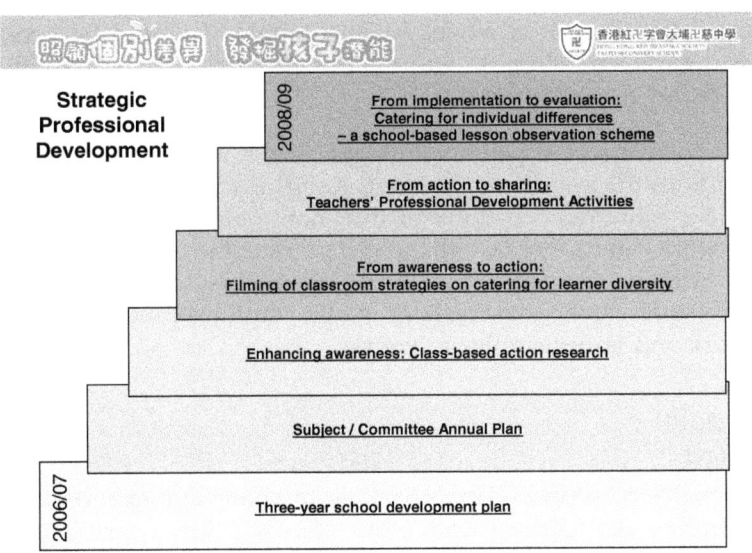

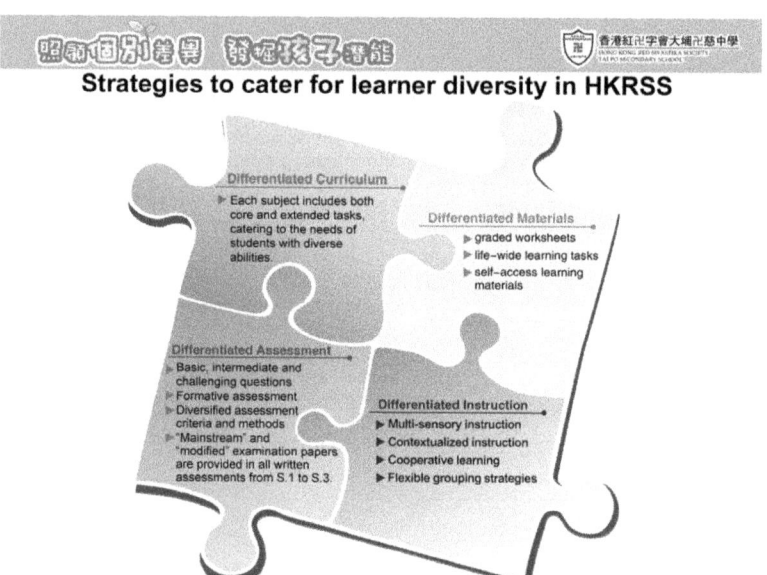

Appealing to international audience

After dialoguing for a while, Angel thought it would be good for Franky to write something to address the international audience of this chapter. Below are her prompts:

> These could be your personal impressions; it might have something to do with the specificity of Hong Kong or the Chinese culture; or also, e.g. what do you think of this: how your resources for doing your work can further be enhanced if you can have an opportunity to meet with or exchange ideas and experiences with school practitioners or researchers overseas or in other cultural contexts interested in work and issues similar to yours?

May 20, 2010
Dear Angel,

Now that I have more opportunities to share our experience with administrators and teachers from other schools, I find a very interesting phenomenon: most schools here in Hong Kong look for quick-fix solutions to their problems! They always ask very context-specific questions, expecting you to give them useful and practical suggestions. However, you can't pick a flower on foreign soil and expect it to grow in your own backyard. Instead of expecting inspiration, most teachers ask for information. I really don't know whether it is a particularly Chinese way of learning. Also, speakers here tend to tell people their experience in great detail without relating it to a bigger concept or a wider perspective. They don't seem to have a habit of generalizing their experience to make it more applicable to other contexts.

I think it may be due to our examination-oriented learning culture as we believe that there is ONE model answer to a question. Also, in our culture, we seem to believe more in authority. Teachers generally don't believe that they can give excellent answers to their own questions without the help of an expert.

Through interacting with researchers or academics, I am under more pressure to subject my experience to greater scrutiny and to generalize principles that could be applied to other contexts. I become more aware of the process of looking for the answer instead of the answer itself. Maybe, a more constructivist approach is needed in teacher professional development.

I am more interested in knowing how school practitioners or researchers overseas perceive, define, face, understand and attempt to solve their 'educational problems'. It is always fascinating to see that some of our biggest problems are not at all their education problems, for example, excessive amount of homework/pressure for primary school students and their parents. However, things that baffle them a lot, such as equity in education, may not be given any attention here in Hong Kong. So, why some issues are considered to be problems in one place but not the other is a very interesting thing for me. Through reading overseas research/literature, not only can I acquire concrete suggestions on good practices, I can also gain an insight into the kind of social contract a society is upholding and defending. Deeper reflection can be done through this kind of comparison, I guess.

Franky

Coda:

Angel's Reflection

When the editor of this volume invited me to work on this writing project with my former MA student, Franky, I thought I could use this opportunity to make the voice and journey of a local school administrator and educator devoted to work for the social justice of children heard and known in the international arena. In the process, I have learnt a lot from the resilient creative agency of Franky and his schoolteachers in overcoming the difficulties in creating a learning space for children with special needs. Reversing the traditional thinking that university professors are the ones who interpret the research literature for students, I enthusiastically echo what Zeichner (this volume) writes:

> Basically, ceding college and university academics the preferential right of interpretation about what counts as social justice in teacher education (SJTE) is inconsistent with the basic tenets of social justice education where teachers and community members whose children attend the public schools would participate in significant ways in the process of shaping and then educating teachers. Some, including myself, have argued that teacher education needs to be situated not in colleges or universities or schools but in a hybrid culture where the preferential right of interpretation is more democratically shared (p. 13).

Having been engaged in this dialogue with Franky, I think that SJTE has to move to a third space: an intersection between the academic's space and the practitioner's frontline experiential space. This intersecting space, which I take to be in the form of a dialogue, has provided me with fresh insights into how academics, researchers, teachers, and teacher-researchers can work together, crossing boundaries in SJTE projects. When we cross our boundaries, each bringing our own unique perspectives, then the result is much more fruitful than we can ever imagine.

Franky's Reflection

Up until writing this line, I have been baffled by a big question: Is this chapter of publishable quality? It does not at all look scholarly to me. I expected that Angel, my teacher, would do a lot of editing to my work in terms of concepts, grammar, syntax and choice of words. To my huge surprise, she didn't. I was left to decide what I wanted to say, how I wanted to say it and why the things I said were important to me. I did not at all feel the pressure to say something that was in line with a certain theoretical perspective. What is amazing about this dialogue is that I can set foot in the academic world and be myself – bringing in the reality that I, as a frontline educator, experience in my everyday life.

Reference

Lin, A.M.Y. (2005) Doing verbal play: Creative work of Cantonese working class schoolboys in Hong Kong. In A. Abbas and J. Erni (eds) *Internationalizing Cultural Studies: An Anthology* (pp. 317–329). Oxford: Blackwell.

Appendix 1

Hong Kong XXXX Secondary School Individual Education Plan

Subject : English   School Year : 2008/2009

Name : _____ (中文)   _____ (English)   Class : S1A   Number :   Sex : M

Special Educational Needs: Reported dyslexic. He has difficulties in reading and understanding short and simple texts. He is attention seeking and refuses to work quietly. He is quick tempered and does not like to follow the teacher's instructions. He does not like to think that his English proficiency is low and wants to work on more challenging tasks but he refuses to spend effort in learning. He needs to have individual attention. He lacks phonic skills.

(Pre-test results: PS1 Attainment Test: (not applicable); He studied S1 in Carmel Holy Word Secondary School. Dolch Sight Words – frustration @ Pre-primer Level; Comprehension: Reading A to Z (RAZ), Level aa: 62.5%; Alphabet Recognition: 100%)

Annual Program Goals: (A goal statement describing what the student can reasonably be expected to accomplish by the end of the school year in a particular subject, course, or alternative program.)

(1) Reading aloud unfamiliar words with all the short vowel and consonant sounds in simple texts (KS1)
(2) Showing a basic understanding of short, simple and familiar texts. (KS1)
(3) Writing short and simple texts with relevant information and ideas (KS1)

Learning Expectations	Assessment Methods	Assessment results
Term 1: 1.1 Revise the alphabet 1.2 Know the 26 letter sounds of the alphabet 1.3 Able to recognize 24 phonemes (RAZ phonics lessons) 2.1 Sight recognize Dolch Sight Words (Pre-primer level) 2.2 Read 26 alphabet books independently 2.3 Read aloud and understand RAZ level aa books 3.1 Use punctuation marks (capitalize the initial letter of a sentence and full stop at the end of a sentence) 3.2 Able to write about one's likes/dislikes/family/friends	1.1 Random recognition of the 26 letters 1.2 Recite the Action Alphabet 1.3 Read aloud; application of /a/, /m/, /n/, /p/, /s/, /t/ 2.1 Read out words on sight 2.2 Read aloud 2.3 Read aloud RAZ level aa Books (1–2) 3.1 Insert punctuation marks – pen and paper task 3.2 After completing a graphic organizer, develop a topic in paragraphs	1.1 100% 1.2 76.9% 1.3 Confused /m/ and /n/; unfamiliar with /a/. Learning progress delayed due to slow start. To date, only completed a, m, n, p, s, t 2.1 Recognized 16 out of 40 Dolch Sight Words 2.2 Cannot apply /a/ in reading 2.3 Unable to remember many words 3.1 Achieved mastery, correct punctuation marks used in written exercises 3.2 Capable of expressing ideas in simple and patterned sentences. Unable to develop a topic in paragraphs
Term 2: **1.0 Phonics** 1.1 Recite the Action Alphabet 1.2 Learn to recognize and apply the following phonemes: o/d/e/h/f/g/i/b/c/r/u/l/w/j/k/v/y/qu/x/z	1.1 Recite the Action Alphabet 1.2 Read aloud; application of the phonemes 1.3 Read out words from RAZ phonics assessment	1.1 Achieved 1.2 Achieved 1.3 With 80% accuracy

Appendix 1 (*Continued*)

Learning Expectations	Assessment Methods	Assessment results

1.3 Able to blend sounds to read out unfamiliar words
1.4 Apply short vowel sounds and learn words using the following phonograms: -an, -ad, -at, -ap, -ot,-op, -ob, -et, -en, -ell, -it, -in, -ill, -ip, -ug, -un,-ut, -ub
 	
2.0 Reading
2.1 Sight recognize DSW (Primer and First Level)
2.2 Learn to read thematic books RAZ levels aa & A
   – Farm animals, Go, Go, Go (domestic animals), pets, baby animals, what lives here, mom and I
   – City, big, little, in, out, in and out, bird goes home (A), going places, up and down
   – Family, on, under, over, my room
   – Summer, summer picnics, winter, spring, spring weather, it is fall
   – Fido gets dressed, my face, my body, getting dressed
	2.1 Read aloud words on sight
	2.2 Read RAZ Benchmark books (levels aa and A)
	2.3 Oral test: Use the action words learned to make sentences
	2.4 Retell 1 story from the materials
		2.1 Frustration at DSW (Primer)
		2.2 Read RAZ Benchmark book (Level aa) with 70% accuracy
		2.3 Able to use 'like', 'can' and 'see' to make sentences
		2.4 Failed

Appendix 1 (*Continued*)

Learning Expectations	Assessment Methods	Assessment results
– The classroom, the school, Maria goes to school – Play ball – The garden, fruit (A) 2.3 Learn action words: we build, my dog, he runs, I can, we can make sounds, what I like 2.4 Active listening to Shared Reading Materials presented by the teacher **3.0 Writing** 3.1 Use 'Wh' words (who, what, when, where, why, how) to organize ideas 3.2 Use graphic organizers to prioritize ideas for presentation 3.3 Write in complete sentences, noting agreement of subject and predicate 3.4 Use proper punctuation: capital letter, full stop, question mark, quotation marks, exclamation mark 3.5 Able to focus on a topic (main idea) and indent for each paragraph, using topic sentences and supporting details	3.1 After completing a graphic organizer, develop a topic in paragraphs 3.4 Insert punctuation marks – pen and paper task 3.5 Write an article	3.1 Unsatisfactory 3.2 Unable to use the punctuation marks 3.3 Unable to write an article

Appendix 1 (*Continued*)

Learning Expectations	Assessment Methods	Assessment results

Term 3:
 1.0 Phonics
 1.1 Revise the Action Alphabet
 1.2 Learn to recognize and apply the following phonemes:
    – Consonant digraphs: ch/sh/ck/th/wh/
    – Consonant blends: br/cr/dr/fr/gr/pr/tr/bl/cl/fl/gl/pl/sl/
 1.3 Able to blend sounds to read out unfamiliar words
 1.4 Able to use the above phonemes to blend sounds with the following phonograms: -an, -ad, -at, -ap, -ot,-op, -ob, -et, -en, -ell, -it, -in, -ill, -ip, -ug, -un,-ut, -ub
 	
 2.0 Reading
 2.1 Sight recognize DSW (Primer to First Level)
 2.2 Learn to read thematic books RAZ levels aa & A
    – Baby animals, what lives here, mom and I
    – Going places, up and down
    – My room
	1.1 Recite the Action Alphabet
	 1.2 Reading aloud; application of the phonemes
	 1.3 Read out words from RAZ phonics assessment
	
	 2.1 Read aloud words on sight
	 2.2 Read RAZ Benchmark books (Level A)
	 2.3 Oral test: use the action words learned to make sentences
	 2.4 Retell one story from the materials	

Appendix 1 (*Continued*)

Learning Expectations	Assessment Methods	Assessment results
– Summer picnics, winter, spring weather, it is fall, fruit, hot and cold – Fido gets dressed, my face, my body, getting dressed, my hair – Maria goes to school, play ball, Maria counts pumpkin 2.3 Learn action words: My dog, he runs, I can, we can make sounds, what I like 2.4 Active listening to Shared Reading Materials presented by the teacher **3.0 Writing** 3.1 Use 'Wh' words (who, what, when, where, why, how) to organize ideas 3.2 Use graphic organizers to prioritize ideas for presentation 3.3 Write in complete sentences, noting agreement of subject and predicate	3.1 After completing a graphic organizer, develop a topic in paragraphs 3.4 Insert punctuation marks – pen and paper task 3.5 Write an article	

Appendix 1 (*Continued*)

Learning Expectations	Assessment Methods	Assessment results
3.4 Use proper punctuation: question mark, quotation marks, exclamation mark 3.5 Able to focus on a topic (main idea) and indent for each paragraph, using topic sentences and supporting details		

Appendix 2
Students' Work
Female Halloween costumes designed by Thomas Tang Ho Yan (2B)

Creating a School Program to Cater to Learner Diversity

First journal written by Thomas Tang Ho Yan (2B)

Second journal written by by Thomas Tang Ho Yan (2B)

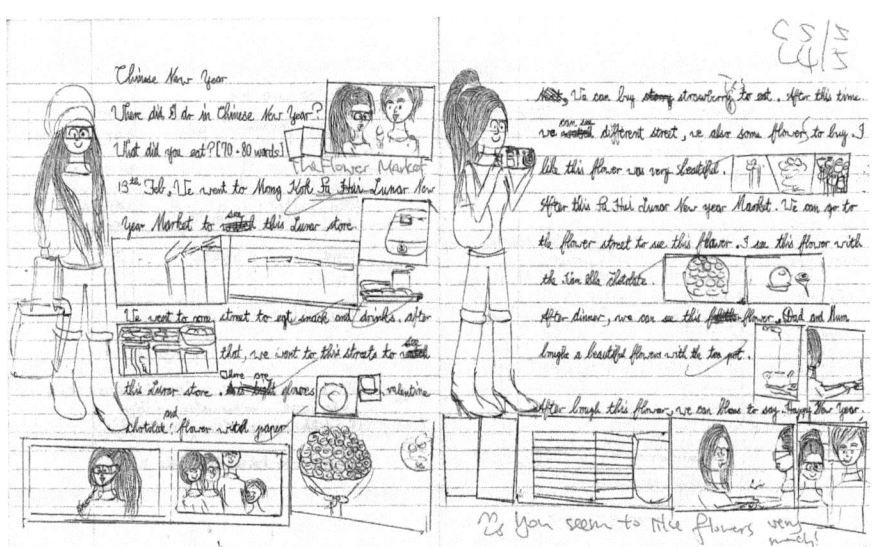

Chapter 8
Working for Social Justice in a Collaborative Action Research Group

KELLEEN TOOHEY and BONNIE WATERSTONE

Introduction

Ken Zeichner's chapter that opens this volume discusses aspects of how North American college and university teacher educators have approached the task of encouraging commitment to social justice in beginning teachers, pointing to tensions between social justice teacher educators and teachers, for example, the tension 'between academic discourse about teaching for social change and the connection of this discourse to communities where the work is to be carried out' (Zeichner, this volume: 13). He argues that one important strategy is for university teachers to form 'strong linkages ... with the teachers and administrators in our schools who are doing good work and with parents and others' (Zeichner, this volume: 18). These alliances, he notes, could not be of the model 'university expert passes knowledge to the uninformed teachers and citizens' but rather, attention must be given to what can be learned from teachers and parents (Zeichner, this volume: 18). In this chapter, we describe a collaborative research group's activities over more than five years, a group formed of teachers, district consultants and university-based others who were committed to social justice and culturally responsive teaching. The group was initiated from a sense of confusion on the part of its initiator, a university professor (Kelleen), who explicitly wanted to learn from the teachers, and this confusion led to disruption of the common practice of university experts telling classroom teachers how to teach, in this case, for equity. Rather, the group was formed with the idea that a dialogue between teachers and university educators might yield insight into the blindingly complex worlds of schools and classrooms and how they might be changed so as to provide, in this case, English language learners with equal opportunities to succeed in school. In time, we came to realize that our group was providing for us an unusual experience, where there was commitment to listen to and consider one another's contributions, and where we recognized that while our institutional positions were different, those differences allowed us insights into perspectives that we could not otherwise have had. We also learned that equitable collaborative relations must be continually negotiated, as hierarchical discourse practices are normal, hegemonic and ubiquitous. Equitable speaking turns are never a 'default position', even when participants are committed to such equity. One of our members, second author here (Bonnie Waterstone), showed in microanalyses that even in such places, the production of power relationships articulate with and sometimes reinforce institutional and structural hierarchies (Waterstone, 2003). In this chapter, we illustrate some of our triumphs, tensions and struggles in attempting to maintain a socially just collaborative action research group, and make observations about how important such initiatives are.

The Teacher Action Research Group

Described in detail in Denos *et al.* (2009), the perhaps inaptly named Teacher Action Research Group (TARG)[1] began in 1999 with several teachers, graduate students (Bonnie was one of the doctoral students at the time), school district specialists, a videoethnographer and a university professor (Kelleen). Over the years of its existence, there were about 10 women in the group,[2] and we met once a week after school, with the initial aim (as I, Kelleen, put it in my research grant proposal) being 'to investigate what practices in classrooms might make a difference to the learning of minority language background children' (Toohey, 1999: n.p.). I had recently published a book, *Learning English at School: Identity, Social Relations and Classroom Practice* (*LEaS*), whose reviewers had asked for more explicit suggestions about appropriate school practices for English as an additional language learners. My three-year ethnographic research in a school was descriptive of classroom practices and theoretically framed, and while I thought that pedagogical implications were implicit in my descriptions, I had not made many explicit suggestions for classroom practice. I was more interested at that point in how researchers and teachers might 'see' classrooms where children were learning English better through the lens of sociocultural theory, and many of my descriptions of classroom activities in the book were deliberately nonjudgmental,[3] partly as a writing technique sometimes strived for in ethnographic accounts, but also partly because I came away from the fieldwork more humble than I had been before, certainly more confused and more impressed by the intricacies of teaching and managing children in the institution of school. I had had a prolonged exposure to, as Zeichner put it, 'the communities where the work [of equity education] is to be carried out', and I was not sure that the 'academic discourse about teaching for social change', at least what I knew of it, would be helpful for telling teachers what to do. I thought that designing improved pedagogical activities would require teachers, as well as researchers, to work together. So, I invited teacher acquaintances, graduate students and others to participate in discussions with me about possible new or modified practices that might help English language learners. One of the criteria I had in mind for the selection of initial members was that I had seen in their teaching, or their writing or in conversations that they were committed to improve schooling conditions for their multilingual students, and their highly diverse students as a whole. Some of these teachers had decades of experience in schools, while others were in their first few years of teaching.

It became apparent quite soon after we began meeting that despite my plans, the experienced teachers in the group were not particularly interested in designing classroom practices; far from following 'a scripted curriculum' that Zeichner (p. 8) warns against, they had had many years of making professional decisions; they created the curriculum enacted in their classrooms. They also rejected the notion that giving other teachers advice about 'best practices' was helpful. Instead of designing or trying out or prescribing classroom practices, these teachers were more interested in fundamental questions about education and schools. Questions such as the following: Who belongs in classrooms? Who has power in classrooms? Do we really want all learners to be 'powerful'? Whose expectations are we assessing when we say that a student is meeting, exceeding or not meeting expectations on report cards? These questions, of course, spilled outside the classroom walls, to engage with larger social, structural and institutional constraints. Given permission, the newer teachers in the group gained confidence to resist pressures to conform to accepted schooling practices (Denos *et al.*, 2009: 53–57). All the teachers wanted to do research in their classrooms, and they were intrigued by the possibilities offered by video recording (which had been used in *LEaS*) to gather data that would help them consider their own questions. The university-based members were also engaged in various research projects. So, over the five years that TARG met, we supported one another with our ongoing, individual and sometimes group research projects.

On the whole, it was a wonderful experience for all concerned, and the group still meets to celebrate its accomplishments: a book (Denos *et al.*, 2009); an article in a professional journal (Denos, 2003); chapters in edited books (Toohey, 2003); one PhD and two master's theses; numerous workshops for teachers and student teachers; academic presentations at American Educational Research Association (AERA) and other meetings; a plenary address at an academic conference; and to keep informed about one another's continuing projects. We sponsored and taught four summer camps for children making videos in 2007 and 2008. We continue to be deeply concerned about one another, and about one another's efforts to make classrooms more just places for all learners.

As we have already noted, throughout the time of our regular meetings we tried to fashion ourselves as the kind of community we wished schools could be: democratic, comfortable with diversity, accessible for all, intellectually stimulating, personally rewarding and actively working to make things better. In many ways, we were that kind of community, and experiencing that encouraged all of us to imagine different relationships in the classrooms in which we taught. However, we think it is mistaken to believe that goodwill, friendship and a commitment to equitable relations of power makes collaborations between university- and school-based teachers always painless or equitable. Rather, power is produced, articulates with and sometimes reinforces institutional and structural hierarchies within such groups (Moje, 1998; Waterstone, 2003). In order to forge spaces where differences are respected and acknowledged, we must understand community not merely as affiliation and alliance. Instead, we believe community building is a struggle and 'genuine diversity must be constantly negotiated' (Denos *et al.*: 114). Before describing our experience specifically, we review some of the literature on action and collaborative research, as most of the research engaged in by teachers in TARG was of this sort.

Collaborative Action Research

> Participatory action research groups come into existence around themes or topics that participants want to investigate, and they make a shared commitment to collaborating in action and research in the interests of transformation. They constitute themselves as a group or project for the purpose of mutual critical inquiry aimed at practical transformation of existing ways of doing things (practices/work),

existing understandings (which guide them as practitioners/workers), and existing situations (practice settings/workplaces). (Kemmis & McTaggart, 2005: 585)

Action research is often described as 'interested research' in which researchers explicitly declare their intention to investigate specific problems in, and improve, a particular practical situation. Nolen and Vander Putten (2007) recently argued that action research was motivated by the perceived irrelevance of most social science research to current real and practical problems; action research, on the other hand, does systematic inquiry into particular problems in specific situations, with the aim of solving these problems. Much action research brings together differently situated participants to collaborate on problem solving, and it often has a critical, political and/or emancipatory commitment (Fals Borda & Rahman, 1991; Freire, 1998).

Kemmis and McTaggart (2005) described action research groups as *'open[ing] communicative space* between participants, [a process which then creates] circumstances in which *collaborative social action* in history is ... justified by the force of better argument' (Kemmis & McTaggart, 2005: 578) (italics in original). Longtime advocates of action research, they see such research as aimed at people searching together for 'more comprehensible, true, authentic, and morally right and appropriate ways of understanding and acting in the world.... It is *a practice directed deliberately toward discovering, investigating, and attaining intersubjective agreement, mutual understanding, and unforced consensus about what to do'* (Kemmis & McTaggart, 2005: 578, italics in original). Kemmis and McTaggart aligned their conception of action research groups with Habermas' (1996) notion of 'public spheres': bodies 'made up of private people gathered together as a public and articulating the needs of society with the state' (Habermas, 1996: 176). Rutherford (2000) summarized Habermas' thought on the success of public spheres as depending on the following:

- the extent of access (as close to universal as possible),
- the degree of autonomy (the citizens must be free of coercion),
- the rejection of hierarchy (so that each might participate on an equal footing),
- the rule of law (particularly with respect to the subordination of the state), and
- the quality of participation (the common commitment to the ways of logic). (Rutherford, 2000: 18)

Kemmis and McTaggart (2005) note that 'Public spheres frequently arise in practice [...] where voluntary groupings of participants arise in response to a ... shared sense that a social problem has arisen and needs to be addressed' (Kemmis & McTaggart, 2005: 584–591 passim).

Collaborative action research has been commonly reported in educational literature. El Haj (2003), for example, described an informal urban teacher network, the Teachers' Learning Cooperative (TLC), in which teachers met weekly to inquire into the political and social arrangements of schooling. El Haj reported that the TLC developed 'a set of oral inquiry processes that use observation and description of the particular as the foundation from which to create rich, innovative curriculum and pedagogy' (El Haj, 2003: 818). She was of the opinion that the inquiry helped teachers to appreciate the profound complexities of teaching and learning. She also noted: 'It is through an analysis of the particular that the conditions that produce inequality are revealed and that practices aimed at social change are developed' (El Haj, 2003: 819).

TARG was, as well, a forum for teachers and others positioned differently in the educational world to analyze particular conditions producing inequality. It was also a public sphere in the Habermasian sense. Access was never policed; members came and went from the group as their schedules allowed, although there was a core group who rarely missed meetings. Because the group was, for all its members, a voluntary commitment, members were autonomous in determining the extent and nature of their involvement. Our rejection of hierarchy (so that members might participate on equal footings) was a stated goal of the group; and we were very largely successful in this, although we discuss in this chapter episodes when hierarchy 'captured' us again. Lastly, of course, TARG did not violate the rules of law (expressed through legislation and policy); although there were certainly discussions in which teachers in particular expressed frustration with curriculum mandated by the province, and policies enacted by administrators and other teachers. TARG functioned as a safe space in which to examine, problematize and resist laws/policies, though not to violate them.

We have not seen much in the action research literature that discusses in detail any of the tensions or struggles there are to maintain collaborative relations of power in public spheres. We agree that such groups have the potential for making deep changes in institutional practices, but we think that it is a mistake to underestimate the power of 'normal' discourse that posits hierarchy and enacts inequities. Like Terdiman (1985), we believe that 'counter-discourse' is difficult and only episodically achieved. We illustrate this belief in the following discussion of not only the triumphs of TARG but also the tensions and struggles within our group.

TARG Research: Triumphs

After about four months of reading and talking together, the teacher members of TARG began to design action research projects of their own. As already mentioned, some of the teachers wanted to use video recording as their main data-collection device, and they also wanted TARG's videoethnographer, Linda Hof, to collect data for them. Linda reminded teachers as they designed their research questions that the video data she would be able to collect would answer some, but not all, types of questions that the teachers wanted to investigate. In time, each teacher articulated research questions, and planned how data collection might contribute to answering those questions. Thereafter, in TARG meetings, teachers individually reported on their progress, shared data, discussed possible means of analysis and challenged one another to deepen their analyses.

TARG's weekly conversations wove together research ideas, challenging questions, discussions of other classroom-based studies and classroom activities through video data or stories brought to the table each week. There was a sense of members being 'of use to each other' – those based in the university and those experiencing classroom life with children on a daily basis. Flexibility and co-ownership of the group's focus encouraged a diversity of projects to emerge, with a common dedication to improving conditions to create equitable classroom communities.

These conversations served several important functions. First, the regular renewing of shared values and visions for practice provided sustenance for coping with the daily stresses of living and working in institutions where social justice was not always a priority. Members rotated through the roles of providing or needing energy and support. The weekly restating of beliefs and perceptions strengthened both the sense of the legitimacy of those understandings and also the resolve to act upon them. A second function of the discourse was to provide language for resisting the dominant practices that seemed so problematic. TARG conversations (like those of the TLC) enabled teachers (and researchers) to 'resist constructing children as successes or failures. ... [,] to consider the institutional structures that resist the child (Carini, 2001) and to imagine changing classroom practices to allow each child's meaningful participation in the community' (El Haj, 2003: 841).

A third function was the exchange of knowledge and expertise. Group members who read, wrote or conducted educational research could add those insights to discussions, and others who spent time in classrooms provided valuable perspectives on constraints and possibilities in those environments. These three functions (renewing values and visions, providing language to resist dominant practices, sharing expertise) supported TARG's collaborative inquiry aimed at improving conditions in schools.

We spent many weekly sessions trying to communicate expectations, to offer alternative wordings and to extend each other's thinking in conceptualizing an inquiry. The conversations within TARG formed a curriculum designed to teach us how to do collaborative research; this way of learning differed from other ways we might have learned – such as reading and discussing written guidelines for how to design qualitative research questions – but that resonated with collaborative research values about joint ownership of the process of inquiry (Waterstone, 2003). As Bonnie put it:

> There were practical consequences of this muddling around—we spent many sessions defining each research focus. ... [but] Our protracted grappling with research design was mediated by and represented our values/beliefs about learning and about collaborative research. (Waterstone, 2003: 57)

Waterstone (2003) used the metaphor of the rhizome to describe the conversational flows in TARG, as we 'muddled through' designing research together (Waterstone, 2003). Deleuze and Guattari's (1987) concept of the rhizome has been explored by curriculum theorists interested in multidimensional, multidirectional flows, and in generative spaces that are 'infinitely complex and continuously changing' (Gough, 2009: 71). The root system of rhizomes is opportunistic, proliferating in diverse directions (think of crab grass, irises, asparagus).

Bonnie noted that in the rhizomatic movement of our conversations, our process of learning the genre of research was multidimensional: feedback came from all directions, and the person describing her research was responding to questions and concerns from everyone present. Kelleen, the most experienced researcher, often phrased her feedback on research design tentatively; Bonnie and the other doctoral student member at the time followed her lead in making provisional or cautious suggestions. But this feedback did not determine the direction of inquiry, as often teachers' comments to each other seemed to be more persuasive (Waterstone, 2003: 67). In reflecting on our conversations, we named this work of collaborating on research design in a more nomadic, less controlled or controllable way as a movement among/between 'shifting centres of expertise' (Toohey & Waterstone, 2004).

TARG action research projects were various. Each teacher developed a research plan of her own, with the understanding that the group as a whole would collaborate in data analysis and discussion. Teacher Corey Denos was interested in how the multilingual girls in her classroom often seemed to be locked in conflict, and she wondered whether teachers should become involved in peacemaking, and indeed, *could* teachers 'peacemake' in effective ways in children's conflicts? Her process of research was described in an article that she wrote in a professional journal (Denos, 2003) and shows how she developed her questions, gathered data, analyzed those data and made tentative conclusions on that basis. By 'analyzing the particular', she was able to understand better the complexity of power relations in her classroom. Another teacher, Susie Sandhu, wondered about how parents of diverse cultural and linguistic backgrounds could be encouraged to participate actively in their children's schooling. Susie's research is described in Denos *et al.* (2009), and it took the form of trying particular activities, assessing them, refining these activities and developing new questions. Teaching English as a Second Language (TESL) specialist Joanne Thompson investigated the 'buddying' program for English as an additional language for students at her school by ethnographically observing two Korean buddies' interaction, and analyzing the discourse in those conversations. Joanne's work became her master's thesis and was framed more academically than some of the other projects.

Some of the TARG research was action research, but not all. Some of our research projects were more typically academic; including graduate theses completed by several members: and journal articles written by the university-affiliated members. All of these products were brought to the group for comment and discussion. Our university members were responsible to their various research communities with their practices and standards of practice, but these projects were enhanced and enriched by TARG discussions.

Cochran-Smith and Lytle (1999) saw school–university collaborative research as challenging traditional educational research by 'call[ing] attention to teachers as knowers and to the complex and distinctly nonlinear relationships of knowledge and teaching as they are embedded in the contexts and the relations of power that structure the daily work of teachers and learners in both the school and the university' (Cochran-Smith & Lytle, 1999: xi). Pappas (1997) also drew attention to the long history of university teachers transmitting knowledge to teachers of children, who, in turn, apply the university knowledge. For her, school–university collaboration in research had many strengths, but dangers of various kinds as well. She cited as problematic issues of validity and reliability, representation of teacher researchers in (usually) university-produced documents and issues of how university researchers can genuinely contribute what they know to collaborate with teachers, without re-instating relations of dominance. Although she did not describe in much detail the latter issue, it was one that had importance for TARG at various stages in our work together. We demonstrate with transcript excerpts two of those occasions below.

TARG Tensions

While TARG members were all teachers and researchers, K–12 schools and universities represent different ways of living in the world – different investments, interests, practices and needs. One example of our differences was that while academics see writing extended pieces for publication and oral presentation of their work as part of their jobs (and more or less welcome), teachers do not necessarily write at length or speak to large audiences of adults as part of their normal practice. Academics most frequently write for and speak to other academics about their work, while teachers are more often in communication with colleagues. Bringing our previous experience with particular practices together as we wrote for and gave presentations to various audiences occasioned tensions and sometimes inadvertent bids for hierarchy.

Our first example of such tension occurred during the first summer after almost a year of meeting in which teachers and the university researchers had completed several projects. Realizing the importance of the knowledge that the teachers were producing, and the enthusiastic reception it was receiving when TARG gave presentations, Kelleen suggested to the teachers that summer projects might be to write pieces for publication. After presenting models of academic and professional publications, the graduate students worked as research assistants through the summer working with the individual teachers on their writing. Suzanne, a teacher, presented a second draft of her writing about how inclusive classrooms operate and what makes an ethic of inclusion transferable to other classrooms. After we read her paper, the following exchange took place:

> **Bonnie:** I thought wow! (whole group laughs) [3-second pause]
> **Corey (teacher):** It's great. I, I just, from the beginning to the end. And I, I think, um, that the changes in the beginning were really effective. I think when you talked about your background in Social Development, it just put the whole thing, the whole thing into perspective and just made all of it make sense. [3-second pause]
> **Colleen (teacher):** I think when you read it, you want to be in your, we want to be in your classroom [chuckle]
> **Corey:** Umhum. Umhum, yeah. It's a wonderful picture of a [classroom], you can just feel it
> **Suzanne (teacher):** [umhum]

Immediately after this acclaim, Kelleen and Bonnie told Suzanne how the paper might need to be changed for publication in an academic journal. We took turns, for almost seven minutes of talk, offering suggestions. Our suggestions were phrased tentatively: 'You could take out some of the evaluative statements you have made about what happens as a result of this activity' and 'One thing I did notice is, um, some repetition, which I think you can, um, take out', but as more experienced writers for publication, our 'suggestions' might have been seen as authoritative. Suzanne had been silent through much of the suggestion time, and her first statement when we wound down was, 'Yeah, I get lost in all the pages, and I don't know, I guess it's a lack of experience'. Suzanne names herself as a novice here, but one of the other teachers in the group went on to cleverly turn the university researchers' words away.

> **Corey:** I just was re-impressed over again ... I keep reading this as a teacher and having been involved in training teachers for a long time. I still read things as if I were a student teacher or I was thinking about giving it to a student teacher, And this [Suzanne's paper] is what I just want to hit student teachers over the head with ... Uh, that it comes with a true belief – that's where the difference is. I mean people can read all the methods and strategies in the world, but unless they really believe down in their guts that each person in the community is valued, and ... that's where the difference in somebody's, versus your [Suzanne's] classroom ... comes in.... I feel like always underlining that, it's so incredibly important. Um, I found from the perspective of reading it as a teacher, and someone who's very interested in training teachers, that the way it's written in a very personal way is very inspirational. And, um ... there must be some kind of places where you can publish this kind of stuff where, you know, your average run of

the mill classroom teacher will read it and ... be inspired by it and say, yes, this is the kind of classroom I wish I had. Um, and if it gets too journalized up then it's not going to be read by those people.

Corey was right, of course: there are such practitioner magazines, teacher federation newsletters and so on, and some of TARG's work was eventually published in those places. At this particular meeting, however, nothing was resolved, and participants went away knowing that something was not right, that we had reached some kind of impasse. We (Bonnie and Kelleen) continue to be embarrassed by our evident overwillingness to jump in and 'fix' a powerful piece of writing.

Eventually, we came to see that much of the power of our work together was because we did not try to turn teachers into academic researchers, or academic researchers into teacher action researchers or try to homogenize the words of university researchers and the words of teachers. Rather, we learned to let our various voices co-mingle. However, the chords we made were not always harmonious. We next describe two examples of episodes of struggle.

TARG Struggles

The tensions described above were somewhat resolved by the variety and multiplicity of publications and presentations that came from TARG: some reaching teacher audiences more directly, some addressed to teacher educators. However, a group such as this, with its commitments to addressing fundamental questions about education rather than designing or prescribing 'best practices', also raised fundamental questions about research, particularly about its purposes and uses. Was research a form of surveillance or exploitation? Who benefits from research in classrooms?

Whether research was sometimes a form of surveillance that only benefited the researchers was a topic on which TARG members did not agree. On one occasion when graduate student Joanne Thompson described her thesis research with a buddy group, Corey Denos asked, 'Does the teacher want to see your transcriptions?' The conversation continued:

> **Corey:** I've never worked with a researcher before, but it seems to me that it would be such an opportunity [for the teacher] to be along with you examining them, rather than waiting to be questioned – did this go the way you thought it was going to go? Puts me [the teacher] on the spot. But if I was actively involved with you every day,

looking at what the data was, then it's a learning experience.

Joanne: To play the devil's advocate, though, if I showed them to you every day, then every day you would go away with some kind of interpretation and you would change what is naturally your behavior. And so, what I had envisioned, was that I would observe for a period of time, and then we would be able to sit down and conference about some things.

Corey: I guess, personally, that feels threatening to me. It feels like you have more power than me because you are observing me privately inside yourself, and not letting me in on the same stuff. It feels threatening to me, so anything you would say would have an extra element, I would feel defensive.

This discussion highlights the difficulties with educational research, as it is often done (by researchers with little or no collaboration with research 'subjects'). While TARG provided a place for teachers to ask these questions, and university researchers to respond, consensus on this issue was not reached. Rather, we lived with this dissonance, with an increased awareness of members' different investments and priorities.

Questions about the purposes and benefits of research were also not easily resolved in our discussions about how to represent our work: who were we writing for, and who are we writing about? As the discussion analyzed earlier suggests, we realized that trying to homogenize the words of teachers and the words of researchers was not a viable option, and so we eventually began to plan a book that would be a combination of stories told at meetings, oral presentations and papers members had written, with a running commentary that (teacher) Corey Denos would write. After an evening of discussion of an early draft that Corey had produced, two members reported back to the larger group that they had noticed that the majority of the classroom stories told about children could be seen as representing the perspectives of white Anglo middle-class women teachers (although not all of us were white or Anglo or middle-class or teachers), and that it would be good in the book to address the fact that we did speak from this perspective – and that naturally, this perspective was limited. They also remarked that there was the danger that the stories could be exploitative of the children and their parents – that is, while TARG benefited from sharing these stories, the benefit for the children and their families might not be so obvious. Some of us agreed or partially agreed with these observations; others did not and felt that 'exploitation' was no part of their intentions in telling these stories, or in what these stories accomplished. Some of those who did not agree were upset and felt accused in a way that threatened their sense of themselves as caring teachers. Some of the teachers had shared their research with their students and their parents and felt that the stories represented children's and parents' voices as well as theirs. This conversation brought up many unresolved issues in our research, and in research generally, and like other researchers who have worried about such issues, we did not develop consensus on how they might be resolved.

In this painful discussion teachers felt misunderstood by other teachers, which was less expected than tensions between university researchers and teachers. The challenges from fellow members raised very emotionally and politically charged issues and opened a rift within the group, but it did not dissolve the group. We are aware that some emotional repair took place in duos. The group as a whole continued to meet, though less regularly. Teachers continued to report on their longitudinal study of and ongoing advocacy for children in their classrooms. The matter seemed to retreat without resolution or consensus and was not directly discussed in subsequent meetings of TARG. Second, although the book project was dropped for a time, it was taken up again; the book was eventually written and published. Perhaps this discussion informed our writing, increasing our awareness of the differences among us not only of our social positions (employment situations, color, ethnicity, gender, age etc.) but also as a result of our differing life experiences and personal circumstances.

In retrospect, as we write this chapter and analyze this moment from our limited perspectives (e.g. neither of us are minoritized women or have minoritized children), we consider that it can be interpreted as an example of the resilience of TARG and the bonds of friendship and trust that had been established; it might also be interpreted as sweeping something difficult 'under the carpet' in order to get on with the work at hand. At the heart of this struggle were thorny ethical questions that haunt any research report or story. From whose point of view is the story told? What differences does that make to the representation? Who benefits from this telling? These are, of course, ongoing issues and we continue to think critically about whose points of view are not represented in, and who benefited from our research in TARG, and in our schools and universities. Along with the differing points of view on research as surveillance, this second example of an unresolved struggle within TARG points to challenges within collaborative action research not often addressed in the literature.

Discussion and Conclusion

We now turn to literature outside action research to analyze the challenges of researchers and teachers working collaboratively toward more socially just classrooms and schools. van der Wey (2007), drawing on Afro-American feminist theory and Aboriginal women writers, argues that the 'hard, uncomfortable and sometimes painful work' (van der Wey, 2007: 996) of coalition building across differences is necessary for social change, despite 'the resistance, tensions, and messiness inherent in such initiatives' (p. 995). Thus, rather than hoping to overcome struggles, teacher/researcher collaborations need to be reframed to understand community as 'the product of work, of struggle ... that has to be constantly reevaluated in relation to critical political priorities' (Martin & Mohanty, 1986: 210, quoted in Waterstone, 2003: 136). Zeichner's call for links 'with the teachers and administrators in our schools who are doing good work and with parents and others in local communities who are working for social change to bring about greater justice within schools and in the broader society' (Zeichner, this volume: 18) needs to be reconceptualized within these more complicated theories about 'communities who are working for social change' as sites of conflict and struggle. There will not be consensus about what 'good work' should be done and how. Rather, differing perspectives about the purposes and products of such collaborations should be expected, and part of the work is to learn how to continue despite unresolved conflicts.

In this chapter, we have shown some of the tensions and struggles within a group formed to create the 'links' between academics and teachers committed to social justice. University-based researchers had different investments and priorities (e.g. in publishing their work or meeting requirements for completing a thesis), while teachers in the group resisted these priorities and maintained that the audience for much of their work should be other teachers or preservice teachers. We seemed to answer the question 'who were we writing for?' by writing for multiple audiences. Our more difficult struggles entailed fundamental ethical questions that arose, even in this collaborative, more participatory research.

Denzin (2000) called for new paradigms of research to address the complex practices and politics of interpretation and inquiry, to not only describe situated worlds well but also to remember that the stories we tell 'should articulate a politics of hope ... [they] should criticize how things are and imagine how they could be different' (Denzin, 2000: 916). The stories told and analyzed in the collaborative conversations of TARG, and the renewal/reiteration of shared understandings, values and approaches supported TARG members in sustaining their commitment to larger issues of social justice through the difficulties and challenges of teaching in schools and, we add, in doing research. We present these tensions and struggles inherent in working across differences, not with a view to offering solutions or resolutions, but with an understanding that genuine community/collaboration entails tension and dissonance. However, it is necessary, and we feel that modeling this kind of 'educative space' in teacher education holds great hope for making things different in schools and communities today.

Our experiences in TARG were characterized not only by tension and struggle but also by triumphs. Our process was complex and messy, conflictual and challenging, but also joyful and resilient. We accomplished a great deal and many of the products of our work were made public, with the hope of influencing teacher education and teachers themselves to enact 'educative spaces' within their own work.

Notes

1. We think TARG was inaptly named because there were more than teachers in the group.
2. A male student teacher was a member of the group for a short time, but the demands of his student teaching and a new family member made it impossible for him to continue. Many of the group members were also parents, and brought that perspective as well to our discussions.
3. We do not believe that descriptions, or any discourse, can avoid expressing emotional attitude toward its content, but in much anthropological text, before a turn to reflexivity, 'non-judgmental accounts' with omniscient narrators were preferred (Clifford & Marcus, 1988).

References

Carini, P. (2001) *Starting Strong: A Different Look at Children, Schools and Standards*. New York: Teachers College Press.

Clifford, J. and Marcus, G. (eds) (1988) *Writing Culture: The Poetics and Politics of Ethnography*. Berkeley: University of California Press.

Cochran-Smith, M. and Lytle, S. (1999) The teacher researcher movement: A decade later. *Educational Researcher* 8 (7), 15–25.

Deleuze, G. and Guattari, F. (1987). *A Thousand Plateaus: Capitalism and Schizophrenia* (B. Massumi, trans.). London: Athlone Press.

Denos, C. (2003) Negotiating for positions of power in a primary classroom. *Language Arts* 80 (6), 416–424.

Denos *et al.* (2003) Dialogues around "Breaking them up, taking them away": ESL students in grade 1 by Kelleen Toohey (1998). In J. Sharkey and K. Johnson (eds) *The TESOL Quarterly Dialogues: Rethinking Issues of Language, Culture and Power* (pp. 87–97). Alexandria, VA: TESOL.

Denos, C., Toohey, K., Nielson, K. and Waterstone, B. (2009) *Collaborative Research in Multilingual Classrooms*. Bristol: Multilingual Matters.

Denzin, N. (2000) The practices and politics of interpretation. In N. Denzin and Y. Lincoln (eds) *Handbook of Qualitative Research* (2nd edn) (pp. 897–922). Thousand Oaks, CA: Sage.

El Haj, T.R.A. (2003) Practising for equity from the standpoint of the particular: Exploring the work of one urban teacher network. *Teachers College Record* 105 (5), 817–845.

Fals Borda, O. and Rahman, M. (1991) *Action and Knowledge: Breaking the Monopoly with Participatory Action Research*. New York: Apex Press.

Freire, P. (1998) *Pedagogy of Freedom: Ethics, Democracy and Civic Courage*. Boulder, CO: Rowman and Littlefield.

Gough, N. (2009) Becoming transnational ... In M. McKenzie, H. Bai and B. Jickling (eds) *Fields of Green: Restorying Culture, Environment and Education* (pp. 67–83). Cresskill, NJ: Hampton Press.

Habermas, J. (1996) *Between Facts and Norms* (W. Rehg, trans.). Cambridge, MA: MIT Press.

Kemmis, S. and McTaggart, R. (2005) Participatory action research: Communicative action and the public sphere. In N. Denzin and Y. Lincoln (eds) *Handbook of Qualitative Research* (3rd edn) (pp. 559–604). Thousand Oaks, CA: Sage.

Martin, B. and Mohanty, C. (1986) Feminist politics: What's home got to do with it? In T. de Lauretis (ed.) *Feminist Studies, Critical Studies* (pp. 191–212). Bloomington: Indiana University Press.

Moje, E. (1998, April) Changing Our Minds, Changing Our Bodies: Power as Embedded in Research Relations. Paper presented at the annual meeting of the American Educational Research Association, San Diego, CA.

Nolen, A.L. Vanderputten, J. (2007) Action Research in Education: Addressing Gaps in Ethical Principle Educational Researcher, Vol. 36(7), 401–407.

Pappas, C. (1997) Making 'collaboration' problematic in collaborative school-university research: Studying with urban teachers to transform literacy curriculum genres. In J. Flood, S.B. Heath and D. Lapp (eds) *Handbook on Teaching Literacy through the Communicative and Visual Arts* (pp. 215–231). London: Macmillan.

Rutherford, P. (2000) *Endless Propaganda: The Advertising of Public Goods*. Toronto: University of Toronto Press.

Terdiman, R. (1985) *Discourse/Counter-discourse*. Ithaca, NY: Cornell University Press.

Toohey, K. (1999) SSHRC Standard Research Grant proposal.

Toohey, K. (2003) Kelleen Toohey responds. In Sharkey, J. & Johnson, K. (Eds.), *The TESOL Quarterly Dialogues*, Alexandria VA: TESOL Press. pp. 92–97.

Toohey, K. and Waterstone, B. (2004) Negotiating expertise in an action research community. In B. Norton and K. Toohey (eds) *Critical Pedagogies and Language Learning* (pp. 291–310). Cambridge: Cambridge University Press.

Van der Wey, D. (2007) Coalescing in cohorts: Building coalitions in First Nations education. *Canadian Journal of Education* 30 (4), 989–1014.

Waterstone, B. (2003). Self, genre, community: Negotiating the landscape of a teacher/research collaboration. PhD thesis, Simon Fraser University, Burnaby, BC.

For Product Safety Concerns and Information please contact our EU Authorised Representative:

Easy Access System Europe

Mustamäe tee 50

10621 Tallinn

Estonia

gpsr.requests@easproject.com

www.ingramcontent.com/pod-product-compliance
Ingram Content Group UK Ltd.
Pitfield, Milton Keynes, MK11 3LW, UK
UKHW021857090326
4719IPUK00006B/1416